So, What's In It For *Me*?

So, What's In It For *Me*?

**It Is What It Is
America's Story Might Be In Crisis,
But Yours and Mine Don't Have To Be**

Michael R. Self, Ed.D.

PALMETTO
P U B L I S H I N G
Charleston, SC
www.PalmettoPublishing.com

Paperback ISBN: 979-8-8229-3908-0
eBook ISBN: 979-8-8229-3909-7

Contents

Preface

Charlsie was a dear friend from our college days. We even graduated from the same high school which might not seem unique until you add in that neither of us were from the town in which we graduated both high school and college. Our town had a population of 17,500 in 1957 and a population of over 160,000 five years later. So the fact we even encountered each other is a story in its own right! She and her husband John became life-long friends, a friendship which endures to this day, with John at least, but we lost Charlsie way too early.

Charlsie introduced me to Story. I didn't know it then, but Story would turn out to dictate how each of us responds to the question in the title. Charlsie loved to shop flea markets. Her garage was filled to the brim with boxes and boxes of flea market acquisitions. I used to look forward to her sharing her latest acquisition's story, which she was always willing to do. She knew the story of every item she ever purchased. She would not buy anything without first being told its story. To Charlsie she was not just buying secondhand items, she was acquiring stories to add to her own Life Story. Her little stories, unbeknownst to her, complemented and reinforced the genetically predisposed Life Story she was living. Her acquired stories helped her continue in the direction her Life Story had chosen for both herself and her husband and family.

I was so taken with her notion of Story I added it to my bucket list of life-long learning topics! I realized early on I was apparently predisposed to be an active life-long learner. Where others might say they were 'led' by God, Fate, Free Will, Determinism, etc., to be this or that I would respond we are most likely genetically predisposed to be such. For most of us rational choices are simply not involved in where and how we wind up where we do, wherever that might be!

Take someone predisposed at birth towards science and subsequently trained as a scientist; to be observant, naturally curious, take copious mental notes, formulate hypotheses and constantly test them. Then, add a lot of teacher, mix in a little social psychologist, stir them together and you have someone with a natural affinity for Story: me. Of course I knew nothing about 'story' in my younger years, I was just living each day come what may. Charlsie helped me finally put a label on an urge or feeling I had always been drawn towards, but which had not sprung forth in any defined direction. Story was that label and direction. Before Charlsie I was subconsciously trying to figure things out about my own undefined story, things which would stay with me for life; some I realized as I experienced them, and others which did not make sense until I was emotionally and intellectually mature enough to process them.

My dad was military so we moved regularly. I attended twelve different schools through high school, four different ones just in the fourth grade! Making friends was out of the question. I lacked self-confidence so success at sports was also not going to happen. Success in athletics is a free pass to fitting in or 'belonging' in any story. Being picked last for playground games and standing alone against the school building during all those recesses negatively reinforced me to become an intuitively good listener and to remember the important aspects about the art of meaningful conversation. For instance, 'How you doin?' might elicit an "I'm good thanks", "Fine, how you doin?", "Not too bad", "I'm ok thanks", or a simple nod of the head. Typically it seems we are on remote response and just blurt out standardized responses regardless of how we might really feel. Too infrequently others might ask how we are and we might respond with an honest "Not well", only to have the inquiring person respond with "Oh, that's good" and then just keep walking on. Most people are on remote control with conversation and just expect the same old response. Most of the time the inquirer is not listening because they are too busy being not 'there', too self-absorbed or just not really connected nor wanting to truly know. Meaningless conversation dominates most human interactions, makes us feel overlooked, not seen and a bit disconnected: alone. This can be changed.

Being a good listener and a good observer go hand in hand. I learned to observe others interacting with each other and intuitively surmised why they were acting and talking the way they were. **Most everyone speaks just to be noticed.** I learned what topics to bring up in any conversation which would allow the other party to be able to talk about themselves. At about the same time it dawned on me that since everyone wanted to talk, i.e., to prove they belonged, to be 'seen', to show they were like everyone else of importance, etc., no one was really listening to each other, and were, as patiently or impatiently as they could manage, waiting for the other person to 'shut up' so they could begin talking to show they 'belonged' in the larger context. I even remember when I had this 'who's listening eureka moment?' I was in the seventh grade and coming in the backdoor of our home from school. As I opened the door, my mother and three of her best friends were sitting around our dining room table enjoying their afternoon coffee and cake. My eureka moment? They were all four talking at the very same time, non-stop. **I wondered, if all four were talking simultaneously, who was listening?** From that moment on I always made it my mission to seriously 'attend' to whomever was talking. Without saying a word I soon discovered I had a growing pool of 'Friends'. A majority of us unwittingly choose our 'friends' based on who is willing to let us do all the talking! That was then and I have tested the veracity of that behavioral axiom ever since. It is as true today as it was then. Cynical, yes … yet true!

A second and equally profound eureka moment for me occurred a couple of years later while heading to get a haircut. My barber was located in a mall and a large group of retirees, all men, would typically gather around the mall's decorative water fountain and sit. (Today you know as well as I do they all meet at McDonalds for breakfast). It struck me as odd: here were men, apparently retired, with nothing to do but congregate in the mall and talk or not, but all of whom seemed to have lost their 'purpose' for living. They were just sitting around talking about the good old days and how today's kids and politicians had gone to heck in a hand basket; sitting around and **waiting to die, because they had no goals left to achieve.** They really weren't 'doin much of anything!' For them the hunt was over!

I swore then and there I would never just sit around waiting to die. I realized I needed to live proactively in every chapter of my life. I was determined my life was going to have meaning and purpose. I had no clue what it would be, but I knew I wanted both.

My third truly significant eureka moment transpired in one of my high school English classes when I first read and then, over-the-years, eventually processed the following quotes by George Bernard Shaw. The first paragraph is from the play *Man and Superman* (1903). The second paragraph comes from one of his speeches (found in *George Bernard Shaw: His Life and His Works* by Archibald Henderson, 1911). Interestingly, as the Internet has a tendency to do, the first and second paragraphs are frequently erroneously combined, as if they were one thought written by Shaw. American actor Jeff Goldblum is quite fond of these quotes and often recites them as one telling.

George Bernard Shaw:

"This is the true joy in life, being used for a purpose recognized by yourself as a mighty one. Being a force of nature instead of a feverish, selfish little clod of ailments and grievances, complaining that the world will not devote itself to making you happy"

"I am of the opinion that my life belongs to the whole community and as long as I live, it is my privilege to do for it what I can. I want to be thoroughly used up when I die, for the harder I work, the more I live. I rejoice in life for its own sake. Life is no brief candle to me. It is a sort of splendid torch which I have got hold of for the moment and I want to make it burn as brightly as possible before handing it on to future generations."

After digesting the quotes I knew that at least one of my destinies was to model my own life story as best as I could along the lines of these two paragraphs. I have since had many more eureka moments in my life, all of which I have also consciously assimilated into my story schema created around the three above 'moments' and a fourth 'moment' I will share shortly in conjunction with James Michener.

There is a concept used by many in the leadership training industry to have their participants write their life story's last chapter first and then go live the rest of their story in a manner which reflects how they want to have lived when they get to the last chapter. In this scenario you write the rest of your story as you live it (hopefully with integrity, meaning and purpose). If you ask most folks what their story is, they will most likely give you an unknowing stare, or maybe offer some reference to money, family, and success as their story. Success though can have a hundred different endings and not all of them achieved with character and integrity. Many Americans do not write their own last chapter, or even their own story; they simply and mindlessly live their interpretation of the American 'Story', or worse have no story at all!. Considerations for a life of integrity, meaning and purpose never consistently enter their life orb! Unfortunately, as it turns out, those Americans who have taken the American 'Story' as their own are in trouble because the American Story is in trouble! It seems the American Story has always been about nihilistic Trumpism. The American Story is no longer about integrity, meaning and purpose, if it ever was, and does not match the last chapter we all thought we were signing on for when we were born into the American Story.

Unknowingly, before I was able to arrive at the point of understanding the importance of writing my own story based on my own personal experiences I was already being shaped by the American Story. The American Story is the story of my/our Tribe, and in our youthful naivete none of us has any control over its power to inculcate us fully into its values, beliefs, and characterizations. It is a tribal and developmental transition from 'Me' to 'Us'. When contradictions arise between 'Me' being who I want to be versus who society expects 'Us' to be, most of us will typically and unquestioningly defer to what society expects of us. The urge to 'belong' overwhelms the urge to be 'myself'! In Freudian terms this is the struggle each of us subconsciously experiences in developing and growing our personalities from Id to Superego, with the Ego mediating. We speak in terms of ego function as the balance between id and superego as our personalities develop.

Unfortunately the American Story does not follow the same storyboard I was creating for myself, and conflict ensued. It would take a Mark Twain to help me properly put everything into its proper perspective. And years later it did as I encountered, fortunately recognized the importance of and adopted as an absentee mentor for my journey into story and storytelling the consummate storyteller, Mark Twain! In later years I realized it was my biological predisposition or affinity for story which drew me to Mark Twain. I have always been captivated by all things Mark Twain. In my preteens I naturally read *The Adventures Of Huckleberry Finn, The Adventures of Tom Sawyer, A Connecticut Yankee In King Arthur's Court,* and skimmed *Life on the Mississippi.* In later years my family took me to Hannibal, Mo. to let me get more into 'character' with Huck. I am one of the fortunate ones to have had the privilege of seeing Hal Holbrock perform *Mark Twain Tonight,* on both live television, and in person at the Saenger Theatre in Pensacola, Fl..

One of my more prized lithographs hanging in my home today, right between one by Norman Rockwell and another by Grandma Moses is the *American Storytellers* by Andy Taylor. Depicted are Will Rogers, Ronald Reagan, Charles Russell, Frederic Remington, Norman Rockwell, Ben Franklin, Ernest Hemingway, Buffalo Bill Cody and Teddy Roosevelt. All of whom are being regaled, under a full moon, around a campfire by Mark Twain himself, comfortably sitting in a rocker. This print immediately drew my attention, not just because of Twain's presence in it, but because of its subconscious pull on my own story; much like Charlsie's acquisitions pulled on her story. If we are receptive, then story is how each of us finds meaning and purpose in our individual lives through daily happen-stance encounters. The Andy Taylor print added to my story, and complimented my search for how one goes about acquiring meaning and purpose. It has reinforced in me that my self-chosen path was the right one for me. Here were storytellers with integrity and purpose.

The only other storyteller I would have wished to have seen added to the lithograph would have been James Michener. Michener and Twain, were the quintessential narraters of the American Story. Michener's works served as the catalyst for my fourth, and maybe most significant eureka moment which significantly impacted my own personal story. During my senior year in high school, 1967, I made it a point to go see the movie version of Michener's 1959 novel *Hawaii*. I had read the book a couple of years prior, and while I was not consciously aware, the novel apparently left a couple of unresolved 'Faith' issues/questions within me. Seeing the movie must have brought my 'Faith' questions back to the surface so I went to my Methodist pastor for guidance and answers. What bothered me most about the book and movie was this question: If the Hawaiian natives had never heard of Christianity, nor accepted Christ as their Savior, wouldn't they still have gone to Heaven? My Pastor's unequivocal answer was 'NO, they would not.'; and therein my fourth eureka moment. 'NO' was not the answer that any God I believed in could support. If there were a God, then He would accept all comers, Believers or not. I wrestled with that answer for years, got the same answer every time I asked it of other Believers, and late in life finally resolved that while I acknowledged an internal intuition towards some sort of 'Faith", I had no use for Man's Religion. I still wrestle with it on a daily basis, but at the time the experience had a major impact on my story.

Turns out our internal intuition towards 'Faith' has biological roots and a genetic component. There is real interest in neuroscience to better understand the brain mechanisms involved when schizophrenics 'hear' voices. The advent of functional magnetic resonance imaging (fMRI) has allowed neuroscientists to record which structures of the brain are 'active' when one hears voices. fMRI studies reveal that a few specific areas of the brain seem to be more active than others when someone is hearing a 'voice'. One of these regions is Broca's area. Another area that seems to be active when someone hears a voice is Wernicke's area which is located at the top and back of the temporal lobe. This brain area is important in understanding speech. Interestingly, there is some evidence that the connections between this region and Broca's area are different in people who are either schizophrenic, highly susceptible to being hypnotized, or a member of the 7-10% of the general population who claim to hear or have heard voices. This is the region which is also active when people claim a 'sensed presence' and the feeling of a 'sentient being', i.e., God or Faith.

In recent years I visited both Michener's Writing desk, located in the Michener Art Museum in Doylestown, PA and Twain's writing studio on the grounds of Elmira College, Elmira, NY; the same campus which houses the Center for Mark Twain Studies. And to bring the story full circle I was honored to be able to thank Twain for his guidance as my absentee mentor by visiting him graveside at Woodlawn Cemetery, and thanking him in person.

Through Mark Twain's perspective I began to see the truer nature of the American Story. America was settled by pioneers and settlers from two different genes pools (temperaments) with the pools themselves dating back thousands of years.

As I will expand upon later, we come into this world alone and we leave this world alone. It is how and what we 'write' in between which will determine whether or not we arrive at the last chapter of our story feeling like we were not so very much alone and we wrote the very best story we could. We will always be alone. We should strive to get to the end of our story being able to look ourselves in the mirror each day liking what we see and satisfied it is an image which values integrity and is proactively seeking meaning and purpose! Regrettably the wholesale, non-critical, unquestioning adoption of the American Story as personal story by so many Americans has proven to not be getting us to that conclusion while looking at ourselves in our 'mirror'! It is imperative we give ourselves permission to look into the mirror and ask the important questions of ourselves. It is Ok to be Ok! Far too many Americans are definitely resigned to being Not Ok!

The title of my personal story is: *He Put Back More Than He Took*. The title will be engraved on my tombstone. The chapter titles of my story, while in no particular order and certainly not all-inclusive include:

Be The Best Listener You Can Be
Be Willing To Compromise
Don't Worry, Be Happy
To Relieve Stress Take Many-Mini Vacations
On The Importance Of Integrity and Honesty
Family And Friends Come First
Life Is Fleeting, So...
Enjoy Each Chapter To The Max As You Live It
Share Your Story With Others
Surround Yourself With Like-Minded Storytellers

You will see no chapters on achieving the American Dream, a hollow dream driven by the acquisition of material wealth, power or status. And so I have been living my story. Along the way I also 'preach' to anyone who might be listening on the importance and necessity of story to defeat the continuation of the impersonalization of civilization. I am human and I am as flawed as any other human, but as I enter my final chapter I am generally content that 'I'm Doin Ok and Thanks for Asking!' Where I am least content is with the turn America's Story has taken and its clearly disastrous effects on the personal stories of those who still manage to care about how they and others are 'Doin'. I love my country! I get teary-eyed at the playing of the National Anthem, would certainly have served in Vietnam if called to serve and mourn to this day for the friends I lost there. While not religious, I am a man of Faith. All of these traits and more speak as examples to the loss of character now lost to the American Story.

Politically I would be considered just left of center. I have some strong conservative views, and some equally strong liberal views. Since I see both sides of hot button issues I have always believed my views, both left and right, made me a political Moderate with no automatic Party affiliation. I remain a Moderate today. I have never voted for a Republican Presidential candidate, but have voted for the occasional Independent one when I deemed them the better Presidential option. I have always seen it as my patriotic duty to vote and have always done so.

And then along comes a spider in the form of Donald Trump who practically single-handedly upset the balance of temperament or dual story lines in America. Prior to Trump, America, while declining, was at least able to hold its 'tolerance' of the other sides's values, be they 'tolerant' of Red America's views by Blue America, or by Red America of Blue America's values and story line. In the 2020 Presidential election 75,000,000 voters announced they were no longer going to 'tolerate', much less be indifferent to, opposing views. Why? Because Donald Trump happened. He publicly flaunted his lying, cheating, womanizing, bullying and false facts, corruption and got away with it. If one's 'leader' flaunts immoral behavior and gets away with it, then his 'followers' implicitly interpret they also have been given permission to do the same!

Donald Trump's public flaunting of, and distain for America's conventional, yet all-the-while ever-changing, cultural values, both good and bad, lanced a two-hundred-fifty year old festering boil of what Mark Twain would refer to as mixed character temperaments. A boil which we now refer to as Trumpism. And while Trumpism might be interpreted as political ideology it would be a false interpretation since Trumpism does not espouse any real political philosophy, other than absolute nihilism. Nihilism is the belief that all values are baseless (… hence 'flauntable and distainable'…) and is often associated with extreme pessimism. A true nihilist would believe in nothing, have no loyalties, and no purpose other than, perhaps, an impulse to destroy. A 'Trumpist' would be the antithesis of Shaw's aspiration to a higher purpose: "a feverish, selfish little clod of ailments and grievances, suffering from overly narcissistic Entitlement and complaining that the world will not devote itself to making them happy; with a character reflective of extreme individualism and willing to destroy the Constitution in order to get what they want to make themselves happy and to prove to no one but themselves that they belong and matter". Trumpism has accelerated the split of America into two distinctly separate countries within one definable boundary: Red America and Blue America; two countries with two different versions of character, Constitution, economics, and American history.

Ken Burns who, rather than Donald Trump, seems to be America's late 20th-early 21st Century's representational figure, much as Mark Twain was recognized as such to late 19th Century America, speaks to the split:

> "This is a simple choice between Bedford Falls and Pottersville: Where does America want to live?…Its just an area where it is important to make it clear that there is no common ground. Nothing lasts forever. There is nothing which guarantees that America will endure. The question is do we wish to be complicit in the end of the American experience?" (Lang, B. (2022), Ken Burns' Urgent Warning: Why He is Scared For America's Future, *Variety*)

Ken Burns, himself a consummate storyteller and widely acclaimed American History filmmaker, is best known for his documentary films and television shows, many of which chronicle American history and culture: *The Civil War* (1990), *Baseball* (1994), *Jazz* (2001), *the War* (2007), *America's Best Idea* (2009), *Prohibition* (2011), *The Roosevelts* (2014), *The Vietnam War* (2017), *Country Music* (2019). After Twain, if anyone best speaks to the importance of Story and Character to a nation it is Burns. And if America as we think we know it from our childhoods does not 'endure', as most think it won't, then the American Story is certainly about to be DOA. Maybe not in our immediate lifetimes, but DOA none-the-less! If the American Story is dying, then each of us is complicit in its loss of character because we have failed to stand up and be seen doing the right things because they are the 'right things to do', regardless of how uncomfortable or challenging they might be to stand up for. The question remains, 'How do those of us trying to write a proactive story in the midst of such chaos endure? Fortunately there is an answer.

The onus for the death spiral of the American Story is on all Americans whether or not we align ourselves with either Red or Blue America, or even if we refuse to align with either and prefer to consider ourselves simply as Moderate Americans. But far-and-away the greater onus for the intentionally nihilistic assault on our collective story has been meted out by Red America. In my prequel to this book, *I Think, Therefore I Am, ... probably wrong*, I set about to discover by **"What thoughtful, dispassionate, reasoned process could anyone go through which would have as its natural conclusion that Trump would be the better President?"** What I found then was a distinction in how the two temperaments (Red/Blue Extreme and Red/Blue Moderate) are really a difference in how people think and make decisions. The two temperaments route decision-making through two different brain structures to make their choices. For the most part the extremes of both Red/Blue America are hyper-reactive decision-makers and make decisions instantly, subconsciously and almost entirely based on what they feel. Moderate Red/Blue Americans are more deliberate, proactive, rational decision-makers. One group routes decisions/actions through the Amygdala (Fight or Flight) and the later routes through the Anterior Cingulate Cortex. Also involved are the Prefrontal Cortex (PFC) which is where the brain settles things. We are 25-27 years old by the time our PFC fully develops. Once this brain part becomes reliable we can look at a situation and consider how things may play out in the future. Unfortunately, as even Piaget acknowledged, for a significant percentage of the population, the PFC probably never fully develops fully enough to be used proactively in decision-making. Also involved in proactive decision-making is the Hippocampus. This structure appears to serve as the brain's secretary or filing system. The Hippocampus notes the associations we make and then reminds us of them when it decides it is the right time.

My focus in this book is directed towards understanding what kinds of stories hyper-reactive decision-makers and proactive decision-makers write and live as Story? Can both types of stories co-exist in one America? How/Why did our reasonably intelligent Founding Fathers attempt to merge two clearly divergent story-lines into one American Story in the first place? Surely they would have suspected the resultant story was doomed from the beginning, even while admitting they were powerless to do anything about it? But most important of all I selfishly want to know how the downward spiral of the American Story into the American Malaise is going to effect my own final chapter of my story, and the life stories of generations after ours? And how is it going to effect all like-minded and non-like-minded Americans? Are there any avenues available in which Red and Blue America can co-exist without destroying each other? Can any of us live proactive lives, full of meaning and purpose, even if others around us are incapable of doing so? Can we ever again ask and then really listen to other's responses on how they are 'doin'?

Years ago I was told I wrote like I spoke: informally and with evident and engaged passion. I was never sure at the time if it was meant as a compliment or not, but I took it as such, and have continued to attempt do so over the years. It is my intention to continue that style in writing this book. I intuited in my early 20's I would be one to embrace the passionate side of Life. It wasn't a rational choice I might have made after reasoned consideration. It just sorta 'happened' and I was fortunate enough to be 'listening' and to embrace it. It was my response to a stirring in my 'Soul?', if you will. It was much later I came across what I had felt for years but then found superbly expressed in somebody else's words: Live Well, Laugh Often, Love Much!

It is easy to tap into the passions within us as we speak, but translating emotions into words is extremely hard when all we want to know is "Why do we behave the way we do?" We are all about our feelings and emotions. We are all about how our feelings subconsciously influence, if not outright make, most of the day-to-day decisions we mistakenly think are rational and consciously made. Most communication between individuals which convey emotions are done so non-verbally and involves decisions about the emotional content of the message having been made subconsciously, and even before the speaker is aware of doing so! Our passions are expressed through our non-verbal cues and messages. The challenge for those interested in putting ideas and thoughts into words to share with others is to translate our passions into words others might equally understand or feel. As I write I have constantly struggled with how formal or informal I should write in hopes of engaging both the emotional and rational processes of you, the reader? Our favorite writers are those writers who speak just to us and who find the words to tap into our own experience base so that we feel the 'passion' with which they write.

While I have paid appropriate homage to Mark Twain for his mentorship and will continue to do so throughout this book, I have come back to this section of my own Preface to share another Mark Twain moment which I ran across *after* I had completed the book. What I have come back to add is a quote from Twain's friend and publisher, William Dean Howell on Twain's 'indifference to narrative form or design'. My own 'indifference to narrative form or design' which I have employed naturally to explain why I write as I speak is my attempt at infusing as much emotion into my wording as I possibly can. William Dean Howell: Clemens 'Was not enslaved to the consecutiveness in writing which the rest of us try to keep chained to. **That is, he wrote as he thought, and as all men think, without sequence, without an eye to what went before or should come after.** If it worked for Twain, I can only hope it might work for me, because this is exactly how I wound up writing even before encountering Howell's quote. Pat Conroy and John Irving could always 'get' to me in a mere few words, regardless of their non-sequential-ness of narrative, because while what they wrote was basically auto-biographical for them, it was also auto-biographical for most of their devoted readers. Their word choice speaks to us personally and taps into our experiences and our reaction to those experiences as we live everyday life!

A second strategy which I unknowingly employed throughout was to not express key thoughts just once and move on to another; instead I employed another version of the application of Twain's 'disruption in narrative consecutiveness'. Twain must have intuited we all have the attention span of a gnat! If Madison Avenue advertisers and tv show producers taught us anything then it is we have to put information out there in snippets, repeat many times and attempt to solve all of life's quandaries in a mere thirty minutes. Journalists of all media types know they have to get all the pertinent information out in the first paragraph-and-a-half or they will lose their readers. After completing the manuscript the first time I also wanted to add the research which supported my 'dis-consecutiveness'. I started with a Coca Cola marketing strategy I had read about many years ago. Their research had shown that a product 'name' needed to be heard at least six times in a commercial in order for the listener to be inclined to go buy that product; in this case a Coke. Turns out the concept has been around from the 1920's and was originated by movie studios in order to get us to buy tickets to the movies. It was called the Rule of Sevens, and is still a viable marketing ploy in today's marketing strategies. Instead of Coke's rule of six, which worked for them, the rule of seven makes sure we hear the product name seven times to increase our likelihood of 'buying' it. If it is important enough to express once it is important enough to share again and again. That is how effective speakers get their ideas across, and is my goal in writing. You will recognize them when you see them. Hence you might encounter a concept seven times in order for me to feel like I might have 'sold' my point.

So, Where Do We Live?

And How Is That Working Out For Us?

A Beautiful Life:
I wish my brain would operate instead of standing still …
…The thread of my own thoughts is disappearing,
to what seems to be a logical conclusion. …
… I've heard a million … reasons and stories
… about this and that …
I guess I didn't like seeing the things I saw.
…'Cause I see, it's a beautiful life
(Don McLean, 1978)

"What did the President know, and when did he know it?"
(GOP Senator Howard Baker during the Watergate Investigation)

Just as easily translates into

"What do we know and when did we know it,
And do we continue to grant ourselves plausible deniability?

"I guess I didn't like seeing the things I saw":

… America is not in its Happy Place!

… Americans are biologically predisposed to be who and where we are: of two Tribes or Stories with each living two differently scripted stories.

… America exists as Red America and Blue America, with two distinctly different versions of itself but trying to live different versions of one story; the American Story.

… America has been Red America and Blue America from its very inception. However, its growth since inception has become its catalyst for reaching critical mass for a catastrophic crisis of Story.

… From its beginning there have been respect-worthy, yet un-heeded voices, e.g., Mark Twain, warning of America's ongoing battle of character.

… The character of the American Story has always been shaped by our various religions.

… There is something off about our Religion; instead of healing and leading the way to American unity, it has become, evermore, the divisive force in pushing all Americans further apart from each other.

> "A broad-minded man, who can see both sides of the question and is ready to hold two opposed truths while confessing that he cannot reconcile them, is at a manifest disadvantage with a narrow-minded man who sees but one side, sees it clearly, and is ready to interpret the whole Bible, or, if need be, the whole universe, in accordance with his formula. (H. Maynard Smith, Henry VIII and the Reformation, 1945)

> Now that we 'see',
> Do we even care?
> But it is never us, is it?
> It is what it is, we say

Religion remains a prominent yet non-proactive force in defining the American Story, just as it always has; fully 66% of Americans believe God was involved in the creation of humans. Instead of writing and living our individual stories around religious principals like the Golden Rule and the Ten Commandments we find ourselves living solitary lives in the pursuit of the American Dream, because the Golden Rule and Ten Commandments have failed us.

How do we know? We all know big homes, fancy cars, nice jewelry, membership in the right church and fortune and fame bring 'successful lives', do they not? We just can not acknowledge the lives full of emptiness and loneliness which comes along with achieving the American Dream? And nothing has come forward in place of religion to fill our lives with meaning and purpose.

Without meaning to come across as sacrilegious, it seems to me that all religious teachings should have been written around achieving the following:

> "This is the true joy in life, being used for a purpose recognized by yourself as a mighty one. Being a force of nature instead of a feverish, selfish little clod of ailments and grievances, complaining that the world will not devote itself to making you happy"

> "I am of the opinion that my life belongs to the whole community and as long as I live, it is my privilege to do for it what I can. I want to be thoroughly used up when I die, for the harder I work, the more I live. I rejoice in life for its own sake. Life is no brief candle to me. It is a sort of splendid torch which I have got hold of for the moment and I want to make it burn as brightly as possible before handing it on to future generations." (George Bernard Shaw)

> And

> "He has achieved success who has lived well, laughed often and loved much; who has enjoyed the trust of pure women, the respect of intelligent men and the love of little children; who has filled his niche and accomplished his task; who has left the world better than he found it, whether by an improved poppy, a perfect poem, or a rescued soul; who has never lacked appreciation of earth's beauty or failed to express it; who has always looked for the best in others and given the best he had; whose life was an inspiration; whose memory a benediction." (Bessie Stanley, 1905)

But it hasn't turned out that way for most of us, has it? Instead it has turned out to be:

> "… a simple choice between Bedford Falls and Pottersville: Where does America want to live?…Its just an area

where it is important to make it clear that there is no common ground. Nothing lasts forever. There is nothing which guarantees that America will endure. The question is do we wish to be complicit in the end of the American experience?" ("Ken Burns' Urgent Warning: Why He's Scared for America's Future", Brent Lang, *Variety*, Feb. 16, 2022.)

If you ask most folks what their story is, they will most likely give you an unknowing stare, or maybe offer some vagary to money, family, and success as their story. Success though can have a hundred different endings and not all of them achieved with character and integrity. Many Americans do not write their own last chapter, or even their own story; they simply and mindlessly live their interpretation of the American 'Story'. Considerations for a life of integrity, meaning and purpose, while periodically acknowledged, never consistently enter their life orb! Unfortunately, as it turns out, those Americans who have taken the American 'Story' as their own are in trouble in the 'Why am I here?" category because the American Story is in trouble! Ultimately the American Story has morphed into Nihilistic Trumpism (the noun). The American Story is no longer about integrity, meaning and purpose, if it ever was, and does not match the last chapter we all thought we were signing on for when we were born into the American Story.

"Huck and Tom represent two viable models of the American Character. They exist side by side in every American and every American action. America is, and always has been, undecided about whether it will be the United States of Tom or the United States of Huck. The United States of Tom looks at misery and says: Hey, I didn't do it. He looks at inequity and says: All my life I have busted my butt to get where I am, so don't come crying to me. Tom likes kings, codified nobility, unquestioned privilege. Huck likes people, fair play, spreading the truck around. Whereas Tom knows, Huck wonders. Whereas Huck hopes, Tom presumes. Whereas Huck cares, Tom denies. These two parts of the American Psyche have been at war since the beginning of the nation, ... and the hope of the nation ... is to embrace the Huck part and send the Tom part back up the river, where it belongs." (George Saunders, *The Braindead Megaphone*, 2007)

The Chapter Last

(From Twain)

Author's Note:

I now share the final chapter of this book, albeit, somewhat out of order? In reality it is the same chapter I wrote as the last chapter of my Life Story some fifty-odd years ago. What I have added in the remaining chapters is the impact living the commensurate 'American Story' has had on my own story. I needed to address how the intervening chapters of my life were influenced both positively and negatively by America's story.

The subtitle of this last chapter is as I wrote it all those years ago: Live Well, Laugh Often and Love Much!

In keeping with the overarching theme of writing one's life story's last chapter first, I extended that concept to the writing of this book. I wrote the last chapter first, then wrote the rest of the book as I came to each chapter/topic. And since I wrote the last chapter first I have placed it in this chronological position, immediately after the Preface and Introduction. MS

Live Well, Laugh Often, Love Much

In 1905 Bessie Anderson Stanley of Lincoln, Nebraska, participated in a contest in which people were asked to answer the question, "What constitutes success?" She won a $250 prize (equivalent to $8,750 in 2023 dollars, so a worthwhile effort) for her response. It was:

> "He has achieved success who has lived well, laughed often and loved much; who has enjoyed the trust of pure women, the respect of intelligent men and the love of little children; who has filled his niche and accomplished his task; who has left the world better than he found it, whether by an improved poppy, a perfect poem, or a rescued soul; who has never lacked appreciation of earth's beauty or failed to express it; who has always looked for the best in others and given the best he had; whose life was an inspiration; whose memory a benediction."

Without my ever knowing it, Bessie Anderson Stanley wrote my last chapter for me, albeit in 1905! All I had to do was live the intervening chapters in such a manner that I might arrive at the end of my story having attempted to fulfill the lofty goals she established for us all with her poem. I always muse: "How 'successful' have I really been?" How true did I remain to living 'The Dream' of a successful life? Would Bessie Anderson Stanley, of Lincoln, Nebraska read my story and subsequently approve of the epitaph I have chosen for my tombstone;

He Put Back More Than He Took

The more astute reader might be quick to say, "Hold on a second, didn't Ralph Waldo Emerson write a very similar-worded poem? His was entitled 'What Is Success'." Your recollection of the Emerson poem would be correct; it has hung on many an office/library wall as an Emerson quote, and is readily available today on the Internet as such, however, he never wrote it! The misattribution most likely occurred in 1911 when Ms. Stanley's poem was the first poem listed in a collection of poems submitted to a literary magazine contest. A poem by Emerson immediately followed Stanley's and over time his name most likely became attached to the poem which preceded his.

Mine is not a perfect story and I haven't always done things simply because they were the right things to do. If my story remains headed in the direction I consciously chose for myself those now-short fifty years ago I will certainly feel like I have been successful. I feel like my life has had meaning and purpose and has been lived with integrity. Admittedly there are still many days I feel empty, alone and fairly uncertain about it all. I still hope Bessie Stanley Anderson of Lincoln, Nebraska might read my last chapter and offer up a knowing smile.

'So how **you** doin?' How 'successful' is your story? We are the final arbiters of our own stories. There are as many versions of successful living as there are people living them. The only criteria to me is how your story measures up to Bessie Anderson Stanley, of Lincoln, Nebraska? I have never given advice, because if followed and proven unworthy,

I lose credibility, and I really value my credibility. Therefore the best anyone ever gets out of me regarding advice is a sharing of how I might do it, but you have to do it however suits you best. And that is my 'advice' for story. My whole point in this effort is going to be to show story is essential to our deciding who we are. Furthermore I will repeatedly stress how all of us are significantly shaped by the larger story of our Tribe. In our case the story of our Tribe is the American Story. And if we are taking the 'advice' of the American Story, we are probably not in a happy place. That story has failed for all the reasons which will be discussed in the ensuing chapters.

> Story shapes our lives.
> It is what it is!
> Story follows its genetically predisposed nature.
> It is what it is
> Story is nurtured positively and negatively by daily experience.
> America's religion has negatively shaped America's Story
> We are, each of us, the American Story.
> Which version of America's Bicameral Story
> have you chosen to live as story?

Where story is involved I always return to Twain for guidance and inspiration. What I 'know and live' from the following excerpt from Twain, is that it certainly seems true we all live for ourselves first, before we live for others. In my living over the past fifty years I have never encountered any substantial truths or behavioral axioms which might challenge the veracity of Twain's 'Old Man's' explanation of our 'me first' nature! We live our lives for ourselves and no one else. Which also means we live solitary lives. That being said, then I must also acknowledge and accept my story is of no significance to anyone other than myself, except for how it positively and negatively impacts on others' lives.

> "This is the law, keep it in your mind. From his cradle to his grave a man never does a single thing which has any first and foremost object but one—to secure peace of mind, spiritual comfort, for himself.

No man has ever sacrificed himself in the common meaning of that phrase—which is, self-sacrifice for another ALONE. Men make daily sacrifices for others, but it is for their own sake FIRST. The act must content their own spirit FIRST. The other beneficiaries come second.

The act must do HIM good, FIRST; otherwise he will not do it. He may THINK he is doing it solely for the other person's sake, but it is not so; he is contenting his own spirit first—the other person's benefit has to always take SECOND place.

Then perhaps there is something that he loves MORE than he loves peace—THE APPROVAL OF HIS NEIGHBORS AND THE PUBLIC. And perhaps there is something which he dreads more than he dreads pain—the DISAPPROVAL of his neighbors and the public." (Twain, What Is Man?, 1962, Ps. 16 & 19)

Again from the Old Man above: "the other person's benefit has to always take SECOND place." If I write for you then I accept that I have written for me first, and for you second. I do so to bolster my notion that those of us who identify as a Red/Blue Moderates can rest fairly assured that in the midst of all this chaos, all this nihilistic Trumpism, we can and do make singular contributions to the quality of life, for ourselves and others who choose to live in Bedford Falls, come-what-may!

We either Live Well, Laugh Often, and Love Much or continue to be the victim in our own life story: We have already made that choice, long ago and our choice was not a conscious one! As I discussed in the Preface Charlsie's sharing of the importance of story only served to put a label on my predisposed affinity for "story". We can be no better or no worse at any given moment than our biology predisposes and our nurturing allows us to be!

The Existential Question, 'To Be Or Not To Be ...'
Has An Existential answer, 'We Already Are ...'.

Ted Danson as Sam Malone
To Dianne as she leaves Cheers for the last time:
'Have A Good Life"

We spend way too much time listening to the negative narrative of the 'talking heads', the conspiracists, the national and local news, our religious leaders and all politicians. Paul Simon's *The Sounds of Silence* lyrics reminds us that while we may have 'heard' it all before, we have now come to 'listen' to way too much of it. Listening shapes our perception. If perception is reality, then our reality is now the negative narrative which is the American Story turned American Malaise. Nobody seems to know how to fix 'it', absent communication and compromise! The pontificators are quick to tell us what is wrong, but rarely offer viable solutions, because for what is really wrong there probably aren't many doable scenarios. The infrequent solutions offered are mostly an afterthought, not very well thought out, and assuredly unrealistic.

My goal has always been to 'live' my last chapter as my viable solution. Write your last chapter first, then write the rest of your story. It is never too late! The solution is individual. Mine is not a solution for society, government, religion, politics, etc.. Mine is a solution for me! That's it. It is what it is. I am not going to advise that you follow my solution. I am going to share it in hopes it might appeal to you in some fashion. Whether you use it or not, while certainly of concern to me, is "none of my business'. My challenge to you is to think about your own story's resolution. Write your own last chapter, if you haven't already. Hopefully your solution will get you through yours.

I Can See Clearly Now:
I can see clearly now the rain is gone
I can see all obstacles in my way
Gone are the dark clouds that had me blind
It's gonna be a bright
Bright sunshiny day
It's gonna be a bright
Bright sunshiny day
(Johnny Nash, 1971)

What A Wonderful World
The colors of the rainbow
So pretty in the sky
Are also on the faces
Of people going by
I see friends shaking hands
Saying, "How do you do?"
They're really saying
I love you
(Louis Armstrong, 1968)

It is a Wonderful World! How do I know? Another excerpt from my story to explain. I have two sons. Both are at this writing in their mid-forties, and until seven years ago, when the youngest married for the first time, neither were married nor showed any interest in becoming so. (It was not until doing research for this project when I discovered their membership in the the previously shared Pew Research Center marriage statistics regarding unmarrieds. In 2021, a record-high 25% of 40-year-olds in the U.S. had never been married. That figure was 6% in 1980.)

Cued by my 'tribal' predispositions it was only natural for me to at least to wonder if either were gay? And if they might be, how would I 'feel' about that? I quickly acknowledged while I might not understand their life style choice, I would certainly love them as much as I always have and anyone they loved would also be someone I would accept into my life and equally love. Having answered that question for myself the more important question, and the real 'purpose' of this project, became: **How does someone else's life-style choice, or color of skin, or choice to have an abortion, or their economic status, or adherence to their church's 'faith statement', or how they choose to pursue the American Dream have *ANYTHING* to do with how I live my life? Their choices have absolutely nothing to do with how I live nor how I strive to achieve integrity, meaning and purpose in my life! Absolutely Nothing! Remember, Mark Twain, through Hal Holbrook angrily and passionately spoke directly to this point when he shared: "Man shall be indifferent to all other religions,**

not tolerant of, but totally indifferent to." Substitute any 'hot button' culture war issue in place of 'religion' and the message is the same: 'Tolerance' implies we are emotionally involved. We probably do not like it nor accept it, but we don't generally interfere; it is after-all the other person's life to live as they choose? 'Indifference' means just that, I am not emotionally involved, nor do I need to be, unless I choose to be and then only in a proactive manner. Trump's very public dismissive attitude towards even the most minimal of social norms and self-imposed restraints simply opened up the flood gates of pent-up frustrations and entitlement on the part of the Far-right Evangelicals.

Samual L. Jackson a la Elijah Price in *Unbreakable*:

You know what the scariest thing is?
To not know your place in this world.
To not know why you're here...
That's... That's just an awful feeling.
(2000)

Seems to me Samual Jackson's adage from *Unbreakable* just drips with irony: a metaphorical statement which embodies a common observation. Aren't we supposed to be engaged by our religion to help us define our place in the world? In reality who would ever consciously acknowledge Jackson's lines as applicable to themselves? But in that same reality, most of us have had at least a moment where we might privately acknowledge what he is sharing?

The relevance of his observation was recently made apparent to me through the content of an online article I just 'happened across'. "Happened across" is something which we all experience, and is story-driven. Apparently our subconscious brains are constantly looking for the visual, auditory and verbal reinforcers which support 'our' version of story as the 'right' story, for us. This is automatic and 'happens' whether or not we are conscious or unconscious of which story we are living. Think about those times you bought a new car, and how all of a sudden all you notice is everybody else with the same car with the same exact color; an example of where others' stories validate our own because we must have made the right choice if so many others made the same choice. We tend to be mega-aware of those events which 'happen' to coincide with our story. They validate the notion we are living the 'right' story; We are not as alone as it might seem sometimes. It is what makes us receptive to life's coincidences.

Mark Twain, explains "happened across" best via his Old Man in *What is Man?* "... Sayest ... the Old Man: ... as soon as a Truth-Seeker finds what he is thoroughly convinced is the Truth, he seeks no further, but gives the rest of his days to hunting junk to patch it and caulk it and prop it with, and make it weather-proof and keep it from caving in on him". Loosely interpreted Twain is saying whichever story we live, we are always looking for support from the environment which reinforces our story. Like seeks like!

John Holmes of Waterloo University further observed that "For better our worse, personal stories are a very powerful source of self-persuasion, and they are highly internally consistent. Evidence [... which we 'happen across' ...] which does not fit the story is going to be left behind [... while evidence which does fit the story will only reinforce it].

The most frequent form of 'happen across' in our lives is music. I have consistently stressed the importance of music to story by weaving it throughout my narrative. I have included a significant portion of the songs which I have spent my '... days to hunting junk to patch ... [my story] ... and caulk it and prop it with, and make it weather-proof and keep it from caving in on ... [me] ...". If one looks at the date of publication of most of those woven lyrics one will see they date back to the time I adopted story as my guide, i.e., "as soon as a Truth-Seeker finds what he is thoroughly convinced is the Truth, he seeks no further."

Southern Cross
I have my ship
And all her flags are a-flying
She is all that I have left
And music is her name
(Crosby, Stills & Nash, 1982)

But what 'happens' when an event does not match our story? What happens when we buy a blue car and everybody else's is pink? The article I 'happened across' was just such a case; it did not 'match' my 'blue car' story, and in the time it took for me to process the article the story had actually become two 'blue car' stories themed to my Live Well, etc., story. The first pink car: Top 10 positive phrases that many Americans hate (Jackson, Ashleigh, picked up by the national news wires, (11/12/2023) based on a Preply survey of 995 Americans). The second 'pink' car was a FB post about removing 'dated' decorations from one's home, with the wall slogan, Live Well, Laugh Often and Love Much being the number one example of dated decorations.

Somewhat tongue-in-cheek, had I missed the point? Could it be me? Per Elijah Price had I misinterpreted my "place in this world? To not know why [I'm] here..." I Am a Truth-Seeker, after-all! My story is about proactive living, so non-proactive stories would certainly catch my eye as an opportunity to check the veracity of my hypothesis regarding the importance of proactiveness to my own life. The scientist in me is constantly testing my hypothesis of story. One should welcome opportunities to assimilate new and contrary evidence, no matter how insecure it might make us feel while we work through it. Don McLean's *Its A Beautiful Life* earworm immediately popped into my brain:

> "Now comes the second verse …
> It's been a long time and
> I'm really insecure about it all"

Ashleigh Jackson's 'pink car': "Meanwhile, a phrase you've probably seen countless times on graphic T-shirts or wall decor was deemed cringy: "Live, laugh, love. About 41% of participants want it banished." (based on a Preply survey of 995 Americans).

And in the second separate 'pink car' article FB has proclaimed my Life Phrase 'Dated?'

Here are the 10 positive phrases that Americans want to "cancel":

- Live, laugh, love
- It is what it is
- Happiness is a choice
- Good vibes only
- Carpe diem
- Find your bliss
- Count your blessings
- Choose joy
- Look for the silver lining
- The best is yet to come

Phrases one, two, and five have always been the heart of my story! How could others be so dismissive of 'my' story? After some consideration and given our penchant for rationalizing away any and all discrepancies it did not take me long to come up with my 'rationalized' response:

1.) Clearly the 41% of respondents who hate the phrases are not using the same definition for the phrases the remaining 59% are using. Like couples in a relationship, or Red/Blue America trying to communicate and reach compromise here is a situation where the same words are being used by two different entities, yet neither has a clue as to what the other is saying?

2.) While the phrases are presented as positive, each could also be construed as a negative put-down. The implication being that if one would just simply apply the phrase to their own situation then life would be so much better? The problem here is we all know we are already doing the right thing, all the time, so how dare others advise me to be more positive?

3.) In Transactional Analysis Theory, people are seen as basically 'OK' and capable of change, growth and healthy interactions. In this model of personal psychology there are four life positions:

I'm Ok, You're Ok
I'm Ok, You're Not Ok
I'm Not Ok, You're Ok
I'm Not Ok, You're Not Ok

As one can see, three of the four life positions have a great deal of Negativity Bias involved and arguably 41% of the survey respondents are living some version of negative life stories and would tend to view life through a negative filter. In the next chapter a great deal of time is spent showing that America is not in a happy place and the responses to this very simple survey are merely indicative of lots of unhappy folks out there.

4.) The second article claiming something is 'outdated' speaks volumes. Interior Decorators make their money by getting us to spend ours to keep up with the Jones'. To claim something as 'outdated' must surely indicate there must be a lot of the 'outdated' item out there indicative of its popularity and place in our culture. More importantly, if one has truly based their life story on an 'outdated' phrase, then that only goes to show the apparent validity of the life style choice in the first place; it has endured.

Ka-Ching

We live in a greedy little world …
… We spend the money that we don't possess
Our religion is to go and blow it all…
… When you're broke, go and get a loan
Take out another mortgage on your home …
… The happiness it brings …
… You'll live like a king
With lots of money and things …
(Shania Twain, 2003)

C'mon guys, we can do this! I know we can!

Well-lived stories based on personal integrity and proactive morality can prevail. By now it should be clear that Live Well, Laugh Often and Love Much has been my personal mantra. My mantra is my guide on how I choose to live proactively, how to better understand others and yet be indifferent when I need to be to why people behave the way they do. My mantra answers, for me, at least, the more fundamental life question regarding "What is my purpose?".

Additionally, I could not have lived my mantra without my music. The 'earworms' I have shared throughout are a small sampling of the life experiences I have 'felt', which like my 'Faith', intuitively match my predispositions to live with purpose. Music has been the glue which bonds my experiences and predispositions to my story. Music has kept me focused on maintaining my integrity of story. Hence the following reflects how I have attempted to live my mantra, then and now!

Writing my Chapter Last (Twain) first and following my own advice:

Live Well: I choose to strive to be proactive. I will always strive to make choices based on integrity, to put back more than I take, consider other's perspectives, and confront my biases. I will always stop to smell the roses along the way and strive to live by the Golden Rule, as it was intended.

Right Living
"Has your's an advantage over the others!"
(Mark Twain, What Is Man?, 1906)

Tin Man
But Oz never did give nothing to the Tin Man
That he didn't, didn't already have
(Dewey Bunnell, America, 1974)

Life is Short
Life is short, Break the rules,
Forgive quickly, Kiss slowly,
Love truly, Laugh uncontrollably,
And never regret anything that makes you smile!
(Mark Twain)

Immanuel Kant
One is not rich by what one owns,
but more by what one is able to do with dignity
(Found in: Richard Dean, The Value of Humanity in
Kant's Moral Theory, 2006)

Chicken Fried

Well it's funny how it's the little things
In life that mean the most
Not where you live or what you drive
Or the price tag on your clothes
There's no dollar sign on peace of mind
This I've come to know
So if you agree have a drink with me
(Zac Brown Band, 2005)

Don't Worry, Be Happy

"Here's a little song I wrote
You might want to sing it note for note
Don't Worry, Be Happy
In every life we have some trouble
But when you worry, you make it double
Don't Worry, Be Happy
(Bobby McFerrin, 1988)

All My Life's A Circle

But I have this funny feeling;
That we'll all be together again.
No straight lines make up my life;
And all my roads have bends;
There's no clear-cut beginnings;
And so far, no dead-ends
(Harry Chapin, ca. 1964)

Reach Out of the Darkness

I knew a man that I did not care for
And then one day, this man gave me a call
We sat and talked about things on our mind
And now this man, he is a friend of mine
(Friend and Lover, 1968)

We All Need a Friend
You just call on me brother when you need a hand,
We all need somebody to lean on,
I just might have a problem that you'll understand,
We all need somebody to lean on,
Lean on me,
When you're not strong,
And I'll be your friend,
I'll help you carry on …
(Bill Withers, 1972)

Laugh Often: I choose to seek meaningful relationships, to work at growing the relationships I do have and to engage with my significant others, family and society.

More Than One Way Home
There's more than one way home
Ain't no right way, ain't no wrong
And whatever road you might be on
You find your own way 'cause there's more than one way home
(Keb Mo, 1996)

War
Why can't we be friends
Why can't we be friends?
Why can't we be friends?
The color of your skin don't matter to me
As long as we can live in harmony
(Charles Miller, et. Al., 1975)

Ob-la-di, Ob-la-di
Life goes on, Happy ever after
(The Beatles, 1968)

Barefoot Children
… We all fell down from the Milky Way
Hangin' 'round here till the Judgment Day
Heaven only knows who is in command…
… But the question's still what are we doin' here
I don't think the answer's close at hand
Barefoot children in the rain
(Jimmy Buffett, 1995)

Its My Life
I don't need you to worry for me, 'cause I'm alright
I don't want you to tell me it's time to come home
I don't care what you say anymore, this is my life
Go ahead with your own life, leave me alone
(Billy Joel, 1978)

We Will Never Pass this Way Again
I want to laugh while the laughing' is easy
I wanna cry if it makes it worthwhile
I may never pass this way again
(Seals and Crofts, 1973)

Love Much: I choose to strive to exercise the highest form of morality and acceptance of diversity. I want to give back to society, to consciously minimize my own negativity, and most importantly learn to love myself. I want to always strive to choose the Greater Good!

Shower The People
Just shower the people you love with love
Show them the way that you feel
Things are gonna work out fine
If you only will do as I say
(James Taylor, 1976)

Let's Live For Today
When I think of all the worries that people seem to find
And how they're in a hurry to complicate their minds
By chasing after money and dreams that can't come true
I'm glad that we are different, we've better things to do
When others plan their future, I'm busy loving you
(The Grass Roots, 1967)

Get Together
Come on, people now
Smile on your brother
Everybody get together
Try to love one another right now
Some may come and some may go
He will surely pass
When the one that left us here
Returns for us at last
We are but a moment's sunlight
Fading in the grass
(Chester Powers, 1963; Released by the Youngbloods, 1967)

BE WELL!

It Is What It Is...

... Seems like a sorry perspective to have towards anything: life, love, work, family, politics, happiness, and religion, don't you think? Almost an indifferent shrug of the shoulder, and rather dismissive? However, I strongly believe the expression very accurately describes the nature of our current lives in the ongoing cultural wars of America and our self-perceived impotence to do anything about it.

... We are, each of us doing the very best we can at any given moment in time. The American Story is as 'good' as it can be, in this moment. While we are hard-wired to function in life to the best of our abilities it is more than likely we have 'temporarily' plateaued in our moral evolution. Life has become, at best, an 'It is what it is' proposition. Too many of us truly believe if we can show others the errors of their ways, or 'enlighten' them, things will be better. Not so, things are already as good as they can be in this moment.

... Trumpism has accelerated the split of America into two distinctly separate countries within one definable boundary: Red America and Blue America; two countries with two different versions of character, Constitution, economics, and American history.

... Americans are struggling to live meaningful lives and the strain of not succeeding is manifesting itself in many of the ways detailed in the next chapter.

The Top Five Regrets of the Dying
"I wish I had the courage to live a life true to myself,
not the life others expected of me,
I wish I hadn't worked so hard,
I wish I had the courage to express my feelings,
I wish I had stayed in touch with my friends,
I wish I had let myself be happier"
(Bronnie Ware, 2011)

This book represents my effort to do something about it. We should, all of us, want to do something about it. If we can not effect the big picture, can we at least do something to show ourselves we are Ok in a Not

Ok world? Not to save the world, maybe, but to save our place in it for having lived successfully in it? I want to have Lived Well, Laughed Often and Loved Much. This is my purpose! My hope is most of us believe in some version of the same. Too many would say they do, when clearly they have not put it into daily practice! I want to know that my life has been lived with universal meaning, purpose and with integrity.

The challenge to achieving purpose is we are all weighted down by the norms and expectations of our Tribal Story, as evidenced by the number one regret of the dying previously shared. We are born into the American Story or Tribe, if you will. Tribe = Religion. Our story is whatever Religion we choose to follow. As we grow we seldom challenge the mores expected of us. We subconsciously buy into whatever values our religion is selling. It makes us incapable of dealing with change involving natural social-psychological evolution. Our Tribal Story (Religion) is not well, and very possibly never has been and we continue to fail to grasp the role religion has played and continues to play in the exasperation of the malaise which is the American Story.

F. Scott Fitzgerald best set the parameters for our challenging times in The Crack-up, a series of essays reflecting his own spiritual and physical decline in the mid-1930's, and published in *Esquire*. Fitzgerald: "Before I go on with this short history, let me make a general observation– the test of a first-rate intelligence is the ability to hold two opposed ideas in the mind at the same time, and still retain the ability to function (which Red/Blue Extreme America has lost!). Fitz continues "One should, for example, be able to see that things are hopeless and yet be determined to make them otherwise. This philosophy fitted on to my early adult life, when I saw the improbable, the implausible, often the "impossible," come true."

I Can See Clearly Now:
I can see clearly now the rain is gone
I can see all obstacles in my way
Gone are the dark clouds that had me blind
It's gonna be a bright (bright), bright (bright) sunshiny day
(Johnny Nash, 1971)

What possible difference can it make in my life if my brother is gay? What is gained if my church adopts a faith statement forbidding gay marriages in my church? Why should anyone's orientation bother me? Where would I think I get my authority to tell women how to best manage their own body's health? Are same sex or inter-racial marriages going to cause me to turn blue and stroke out? How does intolerance of another's religion figure into anything? Why can I not be allowed to contribute and expect rational solutions be applied to gun violence? Where do any of us get off thinking it is our right to manage the moral lives and judgements of others? Certainly societies must and do ascribe to codified laws punishing criminal transgressions against each other, but how has that extended to legislating general morality? We do not have to like or even understand the moral choices others make, but we should certainly be more tolerant and indifferent towards them than we are.

My 'religion' has evolved from our more traditional religious teachings into something akin to Fitzgerald's dual "One should, for example, be able to see that things are hopeless and yet be determined to make them otherwise." The same view which guided the precepts of George Bernard Shaw and Bessie Stanley Anderson:

George Bernard Shaw:

"This is the true joy in life, being used for a purpose recognized by yourself as a mighty one. Being a force of nature instead of a feverish, selfish little clod of ailments and grievances, complaining that the world will not devote itself to making you happy"

"I am of the opinion that my life belongs to the whole community and as long as I live, it is my privilege to do for it what I can. I want to be thoroughly used up when I die, for the harder I work, the more I live. I rejoice in life for its own sake. Life is no brief candle to me. It is a sort of splendid torch which I have got hold of for the moment and I want to make it burn as brightly as possible before handing it on to future generations."

Bessie Stanley Anderson:

"He has achieved success who has **lived well, laughed often and loved much**; who has enjoyed the trust of pure women, the respect of intelligent men and the love of little children; who has filled his niche and accomplished his task; who has left the world better than he found it, whether by an improved poppy, a perfect poem, or a rescued soul; who has never lacked appreciation of earth's beauty or failed to express it; who has always looked for the best in others and given the best he had; whose life was an inspiration; whose memory a benediction."

My religious beliefs motivate me to wonder whether or not we really do come into this world alone and die alone, and if for the most part we actively structure our lives to not be so alone, but we wind up so anyway. I write for the part of me which most-assuredly has Faith, albeit not Faith in man's interpretation of religion. I ask my Faith (that sensed presence or feeling of a 'sentient being' which is evoked when the Broca's area and Wernicke's area are mysteriously stimulated!) to *grant me the serenity to accept the things I cannot change, the courage to change the things I can, and the wisdom to know the difference*.

Secondary to the importance of religion to story, I have always been struck by how important music has been and still is in shaping our stories. Music is mood altering and taps into the memories and emotions within each of us and does so in biologically predisposed ways, both across the culture and individually. Music shapes us. Music tells its own story. Music reinforces the Tribal Story. Music taps the emotive part of our brains. It has long been known that connecting memories with emotion will cause a much stronger retention rate for specific memories. The earliest tribal stories were frequently told through music for a reason; they helped cement the story into memory because of the emotional influence of the music itself. We tend to remember the music which coincides or reinforces our own story on a subconscious level. All the quotes, expressions, and musical lyrics which I have included from beginning to end of my writing are quotes, expressions and songs which reinforced my personal story. Music was to my story what Charlsie's flea market acquisitions were to her story. They were 'outside' reinforcers of our personal stories as we lived them. The fact they made an impression on me served as proof to me, at least, that I was not consciously involved in deciding they were meaningful or not; they just touched my 'soul', and strengthened my 'Faith'.

I have espoused from an early age that music could be, and should be used to build personal relationships and reflect and reinforce our personal values. A quick example: one of the more enduring songs in my life has been Solitary Man by Neil Diamond. The song has been a mantra to me from the first time I heard it. It speaks to me 'A Solitary Man" (I came into the world alone, and I will leave it alone); reinforces who I now understand myself to be, and music is the glue which binds that memory to my emotive subconscious. I have already mentioned that hearing the National Anthem makes me teary-eyed. I am emotionally hooked each time I hear Louis Armstrong's *Its A Wonderful Life* because he is speaking directly to me about my story: a story of love, friends, socialization, mutual support, etc. Hearing *Sweet Home Alabama* by Lynyrd Skynyrd at a football game gets me emotionally involved in the game but more importantly it reinforces my self-concept of who I am and in what I believe. While I have never identified with the darker side of Southern history, I think the song tugs at my emotional identification with more traditional Southern heritage and values, at least to the better qualities of the Southern mystique: manners, charm, socialization, gentility, helping others, a focus on living well, etc. I was never rationally taught to make those associations, but rather they just happened as a part of my genetic predisposition to affiliate with certain aspects of my tribal inculcation.

Frequently song lyrics will spawn an earworm in our heads. An earworm (stuck song syndrome or brainworm) is a catchy piece of music that keeps playing in our head long after the song is over. It is thought earworms trigger involuntary musical imagery in the brain indicating some form of emotional involvement or reinforcement to keep it in the memory. We associate the lyric with an emotional experience. To illustrate: We have the capacity to remember music long after we lose other cognitive functions. Tony Bennett and Glen Campbell both had diagnosed Dementia/Alzheimers. Both continued to sing and perform their music long after they had been incapacitated in other areas of cognitive function. Without necessarily understanding the cognitive mechanism involved in their flawless musical renditions of their 'music', it seems clear there is some powerful connection between music, emotion and cognitive ability/performance.

Everybody's Talkin'

Everybody's Talkin' at me
I don't hear a word they're sayin'
Only the echoes of my mind
People stoppin', starin'
I can't see their faces
Only the shadows of their eyes
(Fred Neil, 1966, Harrey Nilsson, 1969)

Words

This world has lost its glory
Let's start a brand new story..
You think that I don't even mean
A single word I say
its only words and words are all I have
To take your heart away
(The Bee Gees,1968)

Easy To Be Hard

How can people be so heartless?
How can people be so cruel?
Easy to be hard
Easy to be cold
How can people have no feelings
How can they ignore their friends
Easy to be proud
Easy to say no
(Three Dog Night, 1969)

America Is Not In Its Happy Place

Has It Ever Been?

Can It Ever Be?

Don't Sleep In The Subway
You wander around on your own little cloud
When you don't see the why or the wherefore
You walk out on me when we both disagree
'Cause to reason is not what you care for
You try to be smart, then you take it to heart
'Cause it hurts when your ego is deflated
You don't realize that it's all compromise
And the problems are so overrated
(Petula Clark, 1967)

Cool Hand Luke
What we have here is failure to communicate
(Captain, played by Strother Martin, 1967)

Fruitcakes
You know I was talking to my friend Desdemona the other day …
… She told me that human beings are flawed individuals
The cosmic bakers took us out of the oven a little too early
And that's the reason we're as crazy as we are and I believe it
(Jimmy Buffett, 1994)

We Just Disagree
So let's leave it alone 'cause we can't see eye to eye
There ain't no good guy, there ain't no bad guy
There's only you and me and we just disagree
(Dave Mason, 1977)

Even Dolly Parton, the ultimate paragon of virtue, faith, the American Dream and wholesomeness has had ENOUGH:

World On Fire
Now I ain't one for speaking out much …
… I don't know what to think about us …
… God Almighty, what we gonna do …
If God ain't listenin' and we're deaf too …
… Greedy politicians, present and past …

… They wouldn't know the truth if it bit 'em in the ass …
… How do we heal this great divide? …
… Do we care enough to try? …
… Don't you ever believe words don't break bones …
Do we just give up
Or make a change?
… Let's lend a hand … Let's heal the hurt …
… Let kindness work …Let hatred end …
(Dolly Parton, 2023)

America is not in its 'Happy Place'. We stress, worry, overeat, over-spend, opiate and drink ourselves into oblivion. Mostly we are just angry all of the time. We are angry because we are living a Flight or Fight existence as our American Dream. Furthermore we do not even recognize we are so angry and if we do occasionally recognize the effect our anger is having on us we haven't a clue as to why or how to be less angry! We have unwittingly given up hope for a better tomorrow. We spend a great deal of time and money trying to convince ourselves we are happily living the American Dream. We are helpless in acknowl-edging the emptiness inside. We convince ourselves we are living the American Dream, but we intuitively recognize it is a sham, because we are so unsatisfied. So we immerse ourselves in our religion and pretend that the emptiness is no longer there? Our belief in a better after-life allows us to get through this one. We have totally abdicated personal responsibility for leading purposeful lives. Instead we choose to be seen as 'fitting in' or 'belonging to' the Tribe. And we live this way because we have no personal story to guide us through the Dream!

It Is What It Is!

We are, each of us, complicit in our FoMO of the American Dream. We know it is majorly flawed and a dream built on a reality of greed, fractured-right-winged religion, and entitlement, but we are basically ineffectual in doing anything different.

Anthony Anderson:
Too Much?
That's the point!

The point? Our collective intelligence is diminishing. Educating our children has become even less of a priority; we acknowledge publicly that our children will not enjoy the same quality of life we do now. And even if they could, they are ill-equipped to even know how to hold a job to achieve the 'Dream'. Our longevity is declining. We have an opioid crisis which defies logic; we are a nation of drug abusers, prescription and otherwise! We are getting ruder, angrier, and lonelier all the time. We are killing each other in record numbers via another uniquely 'American' cultural calamity: mass shootings. We spend more time alone behind the wheel of our automotive sanctuaries driving in anger about something/anything. It doesn't matter why we might be angry, because we are incapable of simply acknowledging our anger in the first place. Our pent up anger manifests itself in honking our horns, cutting in front of each other at the last second, texting instead of proceeding on through a traffic-light change, racing ahead to cut into the head of the line waiting to merge in traffic. Congress is even considering a national law to ban unruly passengers from flying on commercial flights!

… Sex trafficking. In the United States in 2019, 11,500 human trafficking cases were reported, of which 8,248 reports were sex trafficking.

… Sex scandals abound and while certainly too numerous to list here, include the US Gymnastics abuse cases, the American Boy Scouts, the Worldwide Catholic Church Clergy abuse cases, Jeffery Epstein, Harvey Weinstein, Bill Cosby, and most recently the Southern Baptist Convention's efforts to cover up their sex abuse cases.

… As proof of the influence of the internet in making any and all information available to any side of any argument, I recently 'happened across' a Wikipedia article entitled a List of federal political sex scandals in the United States. How pointed to the American Story that nine(9) Presidents of the United States have had extra-marital affairs and/or children out of wedlock while in office? Sixteen US Senators had affairs; 10 Cabinet level Secretaries or federal judges. Most interesting are the numbers of US Representatives tainted by scandals of extra-marital affairs: Fifty-one (51). Of that number thirty (30) Republicans and twenty-one (21) Democrats made the list. Curiously, since 2010, riding the wave of Evangelical fidelity, the split between Republican/Democrat Representatives in the news over their affairs has a 13/5 Republican/Democrat split.

… Roe v Wade, may have been repelled on constitutional grounds, but the number of states which have now banned abortion are in the majority. Most troubling here is the denial of an abortion in cases of incest, rape and the mother's life being at risk.

… On a single night in January of 2022, over 500,000 people were in some degree homeless. (Homeless under a shelter of some type or unsheltered: Annual Homelessness Assessment Report) As one would expect LA, NYC, Seattle, San Jose, Oakland, Sacramento, Phoenix, San Diego, San Francisco, Denver, Philadelphia, Boston, D.C., and Dallas, have the top ten homeless populations, listed in descending order.

… In 2021 over 48,800 people died from gun-related injuries in America. Mass shootings, defined as four or more injured or killed per incident average almost two per day. In each of the last three years there has been over 600 mass shootings each year. And yet nothing is done?

… The World's best, hands down medicine and medical practices with the worst delivery system to those most in need. Medical expenses account directly for 66.5% of all bankruptcies in America with over $88 Billion in collections.

… Opioid deaths numbered 92,000 in 2020, over 107,000 the following year and are more than 1,000,000 since 2001.

… Suicide in America: 1.7 million people attempted suicide in America in 2021. Over 50,000 of them succeeded. Among 105 Westernized countries the US ranks in the middle for suicides per 100,000 people. 17.7/100,000 for males and 4.5/100,000 for females. The largest percentage group for suicides is middle-aged white men and the elderly.

... *America's Education System Is a Mess, and It Is Students Who Are Paying the Price.* (David Steiner, The74, July 20, 2023). Steiner: The fundamental cause of poor outcomes is that policy leaders have eroded the instructional core & designed our education system for failure.

"What is striking has been the pervasive weariness evident in the commentaries on the results of the National Assessment of Educational Progress. The news was heralded as "alarming," "terrifying" and "tragic." But no one knows how to fix the issues to result in better scores. Diane Ravitch wrote: "Will politicians whip up a panicked response and demand more of what is already failing, like charter schools, vouchers, high-stakes testing and Cybercharters? Whatever the issues, solutions are doubly compounded by the growing teacher shortage. Fewer people want to enter the teaching profession."

Steiner continues, "But these are just symptoms. Factors beyond the schoolhouse door – the legacy of race-based redlining, the underfunding of health care for the worst off, the lack of support for child care and parental leave, and other social and economic policies — remain hugely impactful. The turn away from academics is rocket-propelled by a genuine problem: American teenagers stare at social media on a screen almost nine hours every day, with one result being surging loneliness and depression."

... Americans are 70% ruder today than Americans were in the Sixties. When people 'become' Entitled, they get angry, exude hostility, and assume a stronger sense of entitlement. The person who cuts in front of you in line is often saying: "With the way I've been treated, I shouldn't have to wait in line, too!" We have even stooped to popularizing entire series of tv shows about customer wars, neighborhood wars and courtroom wars? And now we have to contend with Karen moms: mostly middle-aged white women, who are perceived to be racist, entitled or inappropriately angry in public?

...Americans are down on Morality, Family and Country, (Stef Kight and Zachary Basu, in Axios, July 3, 2023).

"Patriotism is on the decline. A majority (60%) of Republicans still claim extreme national pride, but the share has fallen from a near-universal 86% 20 years ago immediately post-9/11. The last time a majority of Democrats said they were extremely proud to be an American was in 2013, months into President Obama's second term. Morality continues to falter. Culture war issues and the debate over abortion rights were at the forefront in the 2024 presidential campaign. New focus on systemic racism after the murder of George Floyd in 2020 — and the subsequent backlash from many Republicans — has helped drive a spike in concerns about racism and discrimination. The so-called "war on woke", led in large part by Florida Gov. Ron DeSantis and aggressively promoted by Republicans at the national, state and local levels, has spurred a record number of bills targeting LGBTQ rights. A whopping 74% of Republicans say the state of moral values in the U.S. is "poor," nearly double what it was two decades ago. The top moral problem, as identified by 18% of Americans, is a lack of consideration of others."

... In 2021, a record-high 25% of 40-year-olds in the U.S. had never been married, according to new findings from the Pew Research Center. That figure was 6% in 1980.

...Years of widening economic inequality with associated increased bodily stress levels are catching up with America: life expectancies have been falling. "After decades of increasing longevity, Americans are facing shorter life spans than their predecessors and their rich-country peers. In states where Republicans set the agenda, it's even worse. According to the CDC, the pandemic accounted for about half the decline in life expectancy, followed by 'Unintentional injuries (16%)', a category that includes drug overdoses, followed by heart disease (4.1%), chronic liver disease and cirrhosis (3%) and suicide."

We are but ...

Dust in the Wind
Don't hang on
Nothing lasts forever but the earth and sky
It slips away
All the money won't another minute buy
Dust in the wind
All we are is dust in the wind…
(Roger Emerson, Kansas, 1978)

… and nothing more!

Life:
Tell me, Life, What are you here for?
Tell me, Life, I wanna know more
Tell me, Life, What are we here for?
Life, go on without me. Take it and you'll see
It doesn't matter. Life, I know what your game is
You take it and trade it. For another Life,
Before you're over, I want something to show for
All my trouble
(Ricky Nelson, 1971)

But this is not all that has America not in its 'Happy Place'.

The decline in life expectancy is also connected to what the CDC calls 'the social determinants of health'; economic policies and systems, development agendas, social norms, social policies, racism, climate change and political systems all figure into the declining longevity of Americans. "Americans with the shortest life expectancies 'tend to have the most poverty, face the most food insecurity, and have less or no access to healthcare," Robert H. Shmerling of Harvard Medical School wrote in October, 2022. "Additionally, groups with lower life expectancy tend to have higher-risk jobs that can't be performed virtually, live in more crowded settings, and have less access to vaccination."

"The highest life expectancies were generally in states on the West Coast, the northern Midwest and the Northeast. Hawaii ranks first at

80.7, followed by Washington, Minnesota, California, New Hampshire and Massachusetts, all with average life expectancies of 79 or higher.

Of the 20 states with the worst life expectancies, eight are among the 12 that have not implemented Medicaid expansion under the Affordable Care Act. The consequences of this obstinate Republican-driven resistance to a program whose expense is more than 90% covered by the federal government include closures of rural hospitals and high rates of uninsured residents." (Michael Hiltzik, LA Times, April 5, 2023)

Mexico
Americano got the sleepy eye
But his body's still shaking like a live wire
(James Taylor, 1975)

… American IQ Scores Have Rapidly Dropped, Proving the 'Reverse Flynn Effect', (Tim Newcomb, Popular Mechanics, April 8, 2-23). A Northwestern University study shows a decline in three key intelligence testing categories—verbal reasoning (logic and vocabulary), matrix reasoning (visual problem solving and analogies), and letter and number series (computational and mathematical abilities). All declined but, interestingly, scores in spatial reasoning (known as 3D rotation) went up. The rise in this one area is out of sync with guesses as to why the other three have tanked, but it seems fairly simple to the educator in me: kids who spend hours each day playing 3D video games are going to be better able to test out higher in questions related to 3D rotation on an IQ test?

…Americans Are Dying Younger—But Where You Live Makes a Big Difference (Jeremy Ney, Time, April, 2023). "The United States is facing the greatest divide in life expectancy across regions in the last 40 years. Research from American Inequality found that Americans born in certain areas of Mississippi and Florida may die 20 years younger than their peers born in parts of Colorado and California. America is unique among wealthy countries when it comes to how young people die, and the trend is only getting worse. Guns are now the #1 killer of children in America and 1 in 25 American 5-year olds now won't live to see 40, largely due to guns.

… Loneliness is now an epidemic, and third leading cause of death in America (Dr. Vivek Murthy, Surgeon Generals Report, 2023).

Lonely People
This is for all the lonely people
Thinkin' that life (…and love…) has passed them by
Don't give up until you drink from the silver cup
And ride that highway in the sky
(Daniel/Catherine Peek, of America, 1971)

Loneliness poses health risks as deadly as smoking a dozen cigarettes daily: the U.S. Surgeon General has said. "Research shows that Americans, who have become less engaged with worship houses, community organizations and even their own family members in recent decades, have steadily reported an increase in feelings of loneliness. The number of single households has also doubled over the last 60 years.

The loneliness epidemic is hitting young people, ages 15 to 24, especially hard. The age group reported a 70% drop in time spent with friends during the same period.

Loneliness increases the risk of premature death by nearly 30%, with the report revealing that those with poor social relationships also had a greater risk of stroke and heart disease. Isolation also elevates a person's likelihood for experiencing depression, anxiety and dementia.

… Pessimism Is the One Thing Americans Can Agree On (Alison Gopnik, *Wall Street Journal*, 2023). Is our glass half-full or half-empty? In research published in Clinical Psychological Science, Gregory Mitchell and Philip Tetlock looked at these questions empirically. Everybody they tested—young and old, conservative and liberal, news-addicted or not—showed the same pattern. Everybody thought that most things had gotten worse, even if they had actually gotten better. Pessimism reigned. The researchers suggest that all of this pessimism may be "rooted in basic aspects of the way we think", i.e., further support for the pervasiveness of Negativity Bias in everyone's life and the need for proactive, personal stories to counteract the effects of Negativity Bias and Flight or Fight Life paradigms!

But let's be honest, we 'Americans" do worry! We worry all the time; we worry about everything and we worry about nothing. And yet we will go to great lengths to convince ourselves and others that we don't worry? We take exception with everything and everybody, any time, any place! We are genetically predisposed to believe everyone is out to get us and everything is a conspiracy (Negativity Bias)! Instead of looking at life as a glass half-full we fret about our glass being half-empty. 'No, never, and maybe' are the first words out of most of our mouths anytime someone makes a proactive suggestion; like the need for some type of gun control or about not having enough money, nor being associated with the right social group. Social media has really given meaning to our FoMO but in reality FoMO existed long before the Internet and has always been integral to Story.

The Evolution of Story

When Story Becomes Religion

And Religion Fails As Story

We now come to the heart of the matter.

Whether we are able to admit it or not, all any off us truly want out of life is to belong and to know we matter. Belonging is the best cure for loneliness. Deep down, without ever really acknowledging it, a sense of belonging helps assuage those feelings of emptiness and loneliness we carry deep in our souls. We need to know we matter. We need to belong so we can have a sense of I Am Ok. The need to belong is not a conscious awareness, a rational choice or decision. Belonging comes from way down deep in our psyche, something driven by thousands of years of evolution and genetic predisposition.

I Am, I Said
But I got an emptiness deep inside
And I've tried, but it won't let me go …
I never cared for the sound of being alone
"I am"… I said, to no one there
And no one heard at all, not even the chair
"I am"… I cried, "I am"… said I
And I am lost and I can't even say why
(Neil Diamond, 1971)

"When we look for the meaning of life,
we want a story that will explain what
reality is all about and what my
particular role is in the cosmic drama".
(Harari, *Sapiens*, 2014)

America
I've gone to look for America…
"Kathy, I'm lost", I said, though I knew she was sleeping
I'm empty and aching and I don't know why
Counting the cars on the New Jersey Turnpike
They've all come to look for America
All come to look for America
(Paul Simon, 1968)

Sounds Of Silence
And in the naked light I saw
Ten thousand people, maybe more
People talking without speaking
People hearing without listening …
Silence like a cancer grows …
(Paul Simon, 1965)

I shared early on we come into this world alone and we leave it alone. What we do with our lives in between determines where we fall on the alone-belonging continuum. I fear most of us can not get beyond the triteness of the expression to ever consider its truer implicit meaning. We say we are social, but not so much.

Fruitcakes
Religion, religion
Oh, there's a thin line between
Saturday night and Sunday morning
(Jimmy Buffett, 1994)

Clean up your own back yard
Back porch preacher preaching at me
Acting like he wrote the Golden Rule
Shaking his fist and speeching at me
Shouting from his soap box like a fool
But come Sunday morning he's lying in bed
With his eyes all red from the wine in his head
Wishing he was dead when he ought to be
Heading for Sunday school, yeah
(Elvis Presley, 1970)

Religion is supposed to teach us the way to fill Neil Diamond's *emptiness deep inside*, but it has failed. We have become the Walking Dead. We attend church semi-regularly not to live better lives, but to network or be seen as fitting in with social expectations. If we 'belong' to the 'right' church, then surely we have met the 'belonging' criteria.

While at church most can never recognize they are just as lonely in church as they were before they walked through the front doors.

We say we want homes with large open kitchens so we can entertain. We build backyard oasis' for entertaining and de-stressing from everyday life but then seldom use either for that purpose. We sit at home on Friday nights wishing for something to do, but then lack the motivation to do anything about it. Many of us try to fill our emptiness void with pets! Having a pet which loves us unconditionally and whom we can love and care for goes a long way towards diminishing our feelings of not belonging and loneliness. Having pets proves to ourselves we matter, because we are responsible for something else, something which depends on us. Before FB and TW we were a country of voracious readers. Why do we read so much? Some of us read to experience 'belonging' through other's lives and experiences. Most of us read to fill up dead time. Sports are so popular because they address three essential predispositions.

They fulfill our need or urge to hunt, to win, e.g. to be the best, and to belong. If my team is a winner, ergo, so am I. It is only as we get older that we typically recognize the wisdom born of experience on just how alone we really are. There is no age demographic more alone than the elderly.

Many of us try to fill the emptiness void with marriage. It would seem that the biological urges which cause couples to fall in love are not manifested for filling emptiness but rather to satisfy the drive to procreate; propagation of the species. Marriage is a social construct (The Seventh Commandment: Thou Shall Not Commit Adultery) intended to encourage mating pairs to remain together to prevent their running around 'procreating' wherever they might choose. Marriage statistics reflect fifty percent of marriages never work. Marriages which persevere most likely do so for either one of two reasons. In the first, two people really do love and complete each other. Even when apart, they are seldom lonely and truly belong to each other. Their completeness or belonging typically lasts well beyond having and successfully raising children.

In the second example couples enter marriage with low or unrealistic expectations. It seems too many of the marriages post-WWII met this criteria. We can say we love each other, and we might eventually, but we can certainly be friends and companions. We do not carry very high expectations for marriage, love or completeness. We marry because society expects couples to marry and have children, and in America, at least, to buy a home and live the American Dream. But at the end of the day, we will most likely still feel empty and alone. These marriages 'worked" but were also filled with a great deal of emptiness and loneliness on both sides. Reasons for the individual loneliness might include: we just kinda drifted apart; our interests were not the same; we just got lazy; we didn't make the effort; I was too tired; my ego was satisfied through my work or through the success of my children in school, sports or careers, etc.. These are marriages which 'work' because couples respected each other enough to be seen as successful by society.

Results from a recent PEW poll highlights the degree of our loneliness and failed marriages: "In 2019, an analysis of census data showed that roughly four-in-ten adults ages 25-54 (38%) were un-partnered". (*Rising Share Of U.S. Adults Are Living without a Spouse or Partner*, Frey, R. & Parker, K. October 5, 2021). Fabiana Buontempo, *BuzzFeed Staff* (An online life style polling blog) used the Pew Data to poll men as to why they do not want to get married. Responses, while not surprising from a male perspective, ran the anticipated gamut: "I grew up around miserable married people"; "The concept that marriage completes one turned out not to be true"; "Marriages around me failed, and those still married fight all the time over petty issues"; "I do not want to get married because I am an introvert and find peace in solitude"; "Marriage is about the ceremony and resulting social contract around having and raising children and less about the compatibility of the partner-bonding"; and "That's a lot of misplaced faith to put into another person".

Reason To Believe
Someone like you
Makes it hard to live without
Somebody else
(Rod Stewart/Tim Hardin, 1971)

Oh, What A Lonely Boy
He was born on a summer day 1951 …
His mother and father said what a lovely boy
We'll teach him what we learned…
We'll send him to school
It'll teach him how to fight
To be nobody's fool
(Andrew Gold, 1976)

FoMO and Loneliness. Yet more evidence we basically live alone: FoMO has also been linked to higher levels of loneliness. Studies of the positive correlation between FoMO, personal loneliness and increased social media use, during and after COVID quarantines, have become more frequent and very consistent in showing higher levels of FoMO-driven use of social networking sites consistently show increased anxiety and higher levels of loneliness in users. For example, Barry and Wong (Fear of Missing Out (FoMO): A generational phenomenon or an individual difference?, Journal of Social and Personal Relationships, Aug. 2020) found that FoMO positively predicted loneliness, and this relation held for both teenagers and adults. Washington State University researchers found FoMO can strike people of all ages. The study concludes that the fear of missing out is more about personal loneliness than what's going on elsewhere in the world.

We should all be living the life Jimmy Buffett clearly lived:

Growing Older But Not Up
Let those winds of time blow over my head
I'd rather die while I'm living than live while I'm dead
(Jimmy Buffett, 1981)

So how does one achieve 'belonging'? How does one minimize emptiness? A life well lived is a life built on conscious attention to building a quality story. A life not so well lived is also built on story; unwittingly followed but a story which most likely lacks purpose and meaning. Story is built upon the stories we experience daily and upon the stories handed down to us which we are genetically predisposed to intuitively identify with (like the Golden Rule, fair play, taking turns, helping the less fortunate, etc.). Children growing up do not know what they might want to be like as adults, but they sure know what they do not want to be like through the unwitting influence of their Negativity Bias. It is akin to going to the grocery store of Life and picking out those traits, beliefs, values, etc., exhibited by others around us for which we have an unconscious affinity to mimic. It also explains why we all have a favorite aunt or uncle; a la Piaget, we are assimilating traits of our aunts and uncles not found in our parents or teachers, but for which we have 'familial predispositions' We just like being around them and do not know why. We are also drawn to the stories of various other 'significant others' as we inculcate (assimilate) our story to match the larger story. Almost everything in our lives is story-driven, or at least affected by story. Quite possibly everything comes down to story. Kim Hamblin-Hart (Making Meaning Of Our Lives through Stories, podcast, March, 2022): "As humans, we are driven to make meaning of our emotions and experiences, whether we know it or not. That meaning comes in the form of our beliefs, perspectives, attitudes, biases, mindset, and the things we tell ourselves. These are called personal narratives. We are story-making creatures, it is a way to make meaning of our life and experiences. It is how we judge things, events, and people in life and how we justify our behavior."

Yuval Noah Harari explains further in *Sapiens, A Brief History Of Mankind,* (in Hebrew, 2011, and English, 2014) Homo sapiens is a story telling animal that thinks in stories rather than in numbers or graphs, and believes that the universe itself works like a story… When we look for the meaning of life, we want a story that will explain what reality is all about and what my particular role is in the cosmic drama. This role makes me bigger than myself and gives meaning to all my experiences and choices. Harari contends that "*Homo sapiens* rule the world because it is the only animal that can believe in things **that exist purely in its own imagination like gods**, states, money and human rights". These beliefs can exact a cost on story though; They give rise to discrimination- whether racial, sexual or political, and it is therefor potentially impossible to have a completely unbiased story or society.

Surprisingly, a life of conscious meaning and purpose is not on everyone's agenda as they travel to their solitary exit. While everyone is genetically predisposed (nature) to story, **everyone's story is not nurtured to consciousness**. Many people live life with little thought to story; these people typically subconsciously adopt the stories of their religion, and specifically the stories of their Bible. Red America is heavily populated with people with no personal story other than believing they live their Bible's version of the American Story. Further they are truly fearful the American Story has moved away from the teachings of 'their'; Bible, and the only way to get 'it' back is to MAGA!

My Life
They will tell you you can't sleep alone in a strange place
Then they'll tell you you can't sleep with somebody else
Ah, but sooner or later, you sleep in your own space
Either way, it's okay, you wake up with yourself
(Billy Joel, 1978)

Alone Again, Naturally
Reality came around
And without so much as a mere touch
Cut me into little pieces
Leaving me to doubt
Talk about, God in His mercy
Oh, if he really does exist
Why did he desert me
In my hour of need
I truly am indeed
Alone again, naturally
(Gilbert O'Sullivan, 1972)

There are no manuals handed out at birth on how to live purposeful lives nor do our parents have a universal instruction manual for getting us onto a path of lifetime integrity and adaptive mental health. Parents intuitively rely on their story to guide them as parents. A small part of their story is made up of how they were parented by their parents, who in turn were parented by their parents. Most parents believe they turned out just fine so intuitively (biologically predisposed) 'know' the proper ways to teach or raise their children. Other parents may take the very opposite view in that they are not going to raise their children they way they were raised. What is happening in these cases is the 'parent' intuitively recognizes that he was raised or nurtured contrary to his instilled predisposed story. Just another example of Negativity Bias at play.

We all spend our entire lives trying to validate ourselves to ourselves and to a lesser extent to others, because we have an innate desire to belong to and be acknowledged so by our larger story, i.e., Red America or Blue America. This is what Joshua Greene addresses in *Moral Tribes* (2013). Tribes are the living breathing Story (with a capital S). We knowingly and unknowingly inculcate ourselves, our children and each other in our specific Tribe's cultural story; hence the expression, 'It Takes A Village!' And the village is the story, the culture; not necessarily specific people. Stories tell us how to act wisely, rightly or wrongly and provide social norms. Stories pass down knowledge and mores. They help us understand each other. The process is called inculcation, assimilation and accommodation. Inculcation is the instilling of knowledge or values in someone, usually by repetition. In today's e-media world, stories are essential in helping us filter out the 'mega-information'. Still, there is too much to filter and we become easily susceptible and vulnerable to conspiracy stories. Storytelling is a fundamental part of being human. To repeat from earlier, John Holmes of Waterloo University: "For better our worse, personal stories are a very powerful source of self-persuasion, and they are highly internally consistent. Evidence that does not fit the story is going to be left behind ... (which for example is how so many otherwise intelligent people easily convinced themselves Trump won the 2020 Presidential election allowing them to easily 'Live the Lie').... Storytelling isn't just how we construct our identities, stories are our identities." We are the American Story. The experiences we have related to story hold powerful sway over our memories, behaviors and even identities. Enough so that we tend to only retain information which fits our story. The American Story is dying because it has become schizophrenic from trying to blend two diverse stories into one unique American Story. One part of the America's Story is now being assimilated into The Red America Story and, separately the remaining part is being assimilated into The Blue America Story. The traditional American Story still has two distinct and totally divergent storylines; the United States of Huck (Blue America) and the United States of Tom (Red America). Both countries are just now openly displayed and waring with each other. Both suffer from lack of integrity, meaning and purpose. Holmes, from above: Evidence that does not fit …primarily Red America's story, and to a lesser extent, Blue America's story… is going to be left behind. We have deconstructed our own historical narrative and are constructing new internal narratives to reinforce our notions of self-persuasion and self-preservation in order to keep our personal narratives 'highly internally consistent'. The reader is most likely familiar with the expression "You are entitled to your own opinions. But you are not entitled to your own facts", credited to either Bernard Baruch (1870-1965), or James Schlesinger (1929-Present), but most definitely to Daniel Patrick Moynihan (1927-2003). Today's dichotomous versions of the American Story are unashamedly written almost entirely with Red/Blue Extreme America's 'own' facts.

"Prior to the invention of the printing press, spoken storytelling was at the core of culture …and often times it was passed down to ensuing generations in song …. It was how histories were passed down, how customs were shared and how traditions became endemic to a group. Shared culture is rooted in a shared tradition of communicating. The stories a group tells meta communicate what a culture values," states Angela Rodriguez (*Storytelling Is a Different Story For Each Culture*, Forbes, Feb 19, 2019). The earliest storytellers date back almost 50,000 years. There is a cave painting in Indonesia which dates back at least 43,900 years and may be the earliest evidence of storytelling. Another cave drawing in Lascaux and Chavaux, France dates as far back as 30,000 years, depicts animals, humans, and other objects. Some of them appear to represent visual stories.

But with the advent of the printing press, stories began to become codified and unchanging. Spoken stories which are repeated and shared in the context of the current storyteller's purview continue to carry the original message of the story, albeit they would match the purview-specific use of nuance, inflection, points of reference, etc.. Prior to the printing press spoken stories had successfully been handed down from generation to generation because the thought, idea, lesson, or moral had not been effected by the syntax of the storyteller. The added benefit of the spoken story was it could continue to grow to fit the times in which it was spoken. Codification, i.e., syntax, directly effects the relevance of story in whichever time period we find the retelling of the story. Syntax directly effects the growth of story. Since syntax is the arrangement of words and phrases in a specific order to most accurately reflect the underlying thought or idea behind it, if you change the position of even one word, it's possible to change the meaning of the entire sentence. All languages have specific rules about which words go where, and skilled storytellers can manipulate these rules to make sentences sound more poignant or poetic. Further and most telling, since the various world religions were the initial, primary benefactors of the printing press they could now decide which stories needed to be codified and allowed to move forward. They could also add new stories to better explain the old stories or lessons, and put everything in the context of the period in which they were being written/codified.

The printing press and the resultant codification of stories in the Christian Bible (the New Testaments), the Quran, the Hebrew Bible (the Old Testaments), the Hadith and Tafsir, and the sacred texts of Hinduism and Buddhism really solidified which stories would be used henceforth to guide moral judgements in various civilizations. Story begot religion and religion begot story. Initially the religious scholars (priests, clerics, mufassirs, lamas, apostles, and imams, etc.) certainly attempted to maintain stories to accurately represent their perceptions of the histories and faiths of cultures and civilizations that exist in today's religious stories. However, as religions suffer from the more frequent fracturing over core values, a little of the original story is lost at each fracturing and hence diminishes its historical story value. Furthermore, what we read today, e.g. in the modern 'King James' syntax, can never accurately represent the original and now mostly forgotten cultural message. Some degree of critical analysis is necessary to approach these religious epics where some stories could have been either allegories or even stage plays but are now probably mistakenly taken literally, as in the case of the Southern Baptist Convention's interpretation of the Bible as literal. Of all the Great Books of Man's Religions the one which has resulted in the most deleterious effects upon its stories is the Christian Bible, specifically as it has been interpreted in America, a country founded on a multitude of fractured interpretations of the Bible!

My Little Town
In my little town I grew up believing
God keeps his eye on us all
And he used to lean upon me
As I pledged allegiance to the wall
(Paul Simon, My Little Town, 1975)

America's Story is assuredly built upon Man's flawed religion, and not God's! If God truly exists, he may have given us Faith, but Man's Religion gave us all the stories we previously used to guide us in living moral and purposeful lives. America was founded on religious freedom so religion has always been a player in shaping the American Story. More importantly it is Man's religion with all of its denominational varieties, interpreted, defined, monitored and implemented by man and not by God, which has failed us all—miserably and inexorably destructively so. Mark Twain was probably the first American to recognize and speak widely to this dichotomy between man's religion and God. Kurt Anderson (in *Fantasyland: How America Went Haywire*, 2017) succinctly details the 500 year decline in man's religion which has gotten America into the moral quagmire in which it now finds itself. Anderson began his own book with the following quote:

"The easiest thing of all is to deceive oneself;
for we believe whatever we want to believe"
(Demosthenes)

'I am the only man living who understands human nature; God has put me in charge of this branch office; when I retire there will be no-one to take my place. I shall keep on doing my duty, for when I get over on the other side, I shall use my influence to have the human race drowned again, and this time drowned good, no omissions, no Ark.'
(Mark Twain, in *Mark Twain*, J. Macy, 1913)

These are the cultural hallmarks of Red America, to wit: More than 6,000 United Methodist congregations — a fifth of the U.S. total — have now received permission to leave the denomination amid a schism over theology and the role of LGBT+ parishioners in the nation's second-largest Protestant denomination. Many of the departing congregations are joining the Global Methodist Church, a denomination created in 2022 by conservatives breaking from the UMC. And the 'good works' of the Southern Baptist Convention? With over 40,000 congregations and an increasing decline in its own 13 million membership and with its own sex abuse coverup being exposed, the church has decided to focus on expelling those handful of SBC churches who employ women pastors, which is against the SBC's statement of faith.

Religion is not a modern-day phenomenon or influencer on story because we now know it has existed since even before the inception of America. According to Julian Jaynes (*The Origin of Consciousness in the Breakdown of the Bicameral Mind*, Boston: Houghton Mifflin, 1976) the advent of religion coincides with the awakening of 'consciousness' in Man. With consciousness comes an awareness of the availability of options and choices in the development of moral culture. Shamans assumed the role of 'interpreting' visions and guiding or telling their flocks what the voices in their heads really meant, and that 'interpretation' still exists today in the form of ministerial interpreters of the Bible and of God's intentions. The best example of how this might have been achieved would be the Ten Commandments. This guidance, both good and bad became codified in the stories handed down from generation to generation, wherein followers eventually came to not question the origin or purpose of Story; they simply complied. America was founded upon a religious freedom which evolved into a darker form than anyone could have ever anticipated. Religion was the major theme of most of Mark Twain's commentaries on the negative, self-destructive condition of America's Character.

Whatever happened to Matthew 7:1: Do not judge, or you too will be judged? What about Matthew 7:12: In everything, do to others what you would have them do to you. This is the hallowed Golden Rule and a foundational, fundamental tenet of the American Story! What has happened to it: It certainly seems dead in modern day America!

Frail Grasp On The Big Picture
And we pray to our Lord
Who we know is American
He reigns from on high
He speaks to us through middlemen
And he shepherds his flock
We sing out and we praise His name
He supports us in war
He presides over football games
And the right will prevail
All our troubles shall be resolved
We have faith in the Lord
Unless there's money or sex involved
(Henley/Frey, 2007)

As best as I can tell God was undefeated
in all sports last year! Anybody who won thanked him
and I never heard a single loser blame him.
(Lewis Grizzard)

Will Rogers:
We will never have true civilization
until we have learned to recognize
the rights of others.

The Necessity of Story

Everyone has a story, purposeful, or not!

Everyone lives their story, knowingly or unknowingly.

Everyone's story is genetically predisposed to follow a specific, unique script with tweaks here and there from one's nurturing.

Through all the eons of time in which stories have been scripted by our genes, two primary story lines have endured and within each exists a multitude of mini-versions of story. However all stories adhere to the major tenets of the larger two stories and have been variously described over the eons:

> "Some scholars assert that the great explosion of human culture some tens of thousands of years ago created the basis for two politically very different types of human. The first ("traditional warriors" or conservatives) reflects the state of the species prior to the great cultural flowering and the latter ("new villagers" or liberals) reflects the status after. The implications are that conservatives are somewhat out of step with current sensibilities." (Hibbing. J.R., et.al., *Predisposed*, p. 17, 2014)

> "Nineteenth-century philosopher John Stuart Mill called it "commonplace" to have "a party of order or stability and a party of progress or reform." Ralph Waldo Emerson noted that "the two parties which divide the state, the party of conservatism and that of innovation, are very old, and have disputed the possession of the world ever since it was made." Emerson called this division "primal" and argued that "such an irreconcilable antagonism, of course, must have a correspondent depth of seat in the human condition. (Hibbing, J.R., et.al., *Predisposed*, p. 17, 2014.

> "Liberals and conservatives often are reluctant to accept that their differences are rooted in psychology, let alone biology. Their own political beliefs seem so sensible,

rational, and correct that they have difficulty believing that other people, if given full information and protected from nefarious and artificial influences, would arrive at different beliefs. (Hibbing, J.R., et.al., *Predisposed*, p. 17, 2014.)

Jonathan Haidt reminds us that historians frequently quote President James Madison's comments in "Federalist No. 10" on the innate human proclivity toward 'faction' (I.e., Red vs Blue America). Madison addressed the evils of our current-day factionalism from a different time period in American history:

"By a faction I understand a number of citizens, whether amounting to a majority …(as in today's social media driven reality)…or minority of the whole, who are united and actuated by some common impulse of passion … (MAGA/Trumpism)…, or of interest, adverse to the rights of other citizens, or to the permanent and aggregate interests of the community. … where no substantial occasion presents itself, the most frivolous and fanciful distinctions have been sufficient to kindle their unfriendly passions and excite their most violent conflicts" …(The January 6th Insurrection, the Big Steal, Over-turning Roe v Wade)… [James Madison, Federalist #10, in The Federalist, 1788]

Additional examples of the dichotomization:

Saunders' The United States of Huck or the United States of Tom?

Burns' choice on where to live: Bedford Falls or Pottersville?

Twain's distinguishing Americans as of two temperaments regarding America's Character.

It would seem all story lines essentially evolved along one of two brain-based decision-making paradigms. One paradigm presents as rational, non-emotive, more methodical and hence slower. This method fosters more proactive scripting of story. Choices are made more from conscious awareness and not subconsciously. This paradigm routes through the Anterior Cingulate Cortex (ACC) of the brain and while it seems to be affiliated with basic survival it takes advantage of rational choices on how to improve upon one's hunting and surviving. The second story-scripting paradigm is based on maximum survival response, i.e., Fight or Flight. It routes through the Amygdala and has evolved over time commensurate with a strong Negativity Bias. Negativity Bias is a highly developed innate negative-attention-focusing process which discerns negative elements and warns us of dangers in our environment. It is our intuitive second-sense on how to avoid elimination in the hunt for food and survival. Negativity Bias alerts to the negative cues in our environment, and can manifest itself as a belief in conspiracy theories where-in others are out to get us. Negativity Bias can be equated to the 'my glass is half-empty' view-point towards life, as opposed to the view that our glass is half-full. Research points to a correlation between political affiliation and Negativity Bas, where conservatives are more sensitive to negative stimuli and therefore tend to lean towards right-leaning ideology which considers threat reduction and social-order to be its main focus. Individuals with lower negativity bias tend to lean towards more moderate political policies such as pluralism and are accepting of diverse social groups which in their own right and by proxy could threaten social structure and cause greater risk of unrest. The fight or flight response to danger or change, is hyper-reactive, emotional, and lightening quick. It makes decisions instantly (200 times faster than rational decision-making) and without our conscious awareness. It is only through conscious nurturing or cultural interference that story lines can go off-script or change.

So, do we manage our story, or does it manage us? There certainly seems to be ample evidence our stories manage us, given most of us live and die never having questioned our story or evaluating how well we may or may not have fulfilled our purpose.

The simplest bare bones version of all stories, stripped of all cultural overlays for both hyper-reactive and proactive stories continues to be: we are born, we mature, we have babies, we live some more and we die.

We are no different in that regard than honey bees, bison, sunflowers, whales, in fact, most all life. And in its simplest version, genetically established and manifested over eons, each of us has a specific role: Procreation. This instinctual, base, predisposition to procreate is what drives the intense emotional reaction of Pro-Lifers against abortion. This is what Mark Twain was telling us through his Old Man in What Is Man?

> "From the cradle to his grave a man never does a single thing which has any first and foremost object but one—to secure peace of mind, spiritual comfort, for **himself**."

Pro-Choice advocates, without even being aware of it majorly threaten the very existence and purpose of story for individuals who advocate for Pro-Life. Pro-Lifers, while assuredly concerned about unborn fetuses are reacting more to their own fears they may have 'followed' the wrong story line; resulting in personal lives lacking in meaning and purpose!

As pairs gathered into communities and communities into societies there was a need to codify societal rules, roles, expectations towards each other, and morality. These became Tribal codes, analogous to various versions of the Ten Commandments, if you will. Eventually tribes merged and blended with each other until there were basically just two predominant moral-driven tribes. These two major over-arching tribes are too often mistakenly referred to as conservative and liberal tribes. They should not be seen, as they typically are, as conservative or liberal in terms of political leanings, but perhaps better viewed as a proactive, rational leaning, glass half-full tribe vs a hyper-reactive, emotive, glass-half empty tribe in their respective outlooks towards life, with untold numbers of tribal variations blurring the boundaries between the two.

Over the eons, stories were codified into expectations and mores on how people were expected to act if they wanted to remain a part of their Tribe. Richard Bach in *Jonathan Livingston Seagull* (1970) provided the quintessential allegory on the power and influence of story. His story shows how the seagull flock is guided by its Elder's laying down the law (Religion). One dare not violate the law (Religion) in the name of individuality, lest they become outcasts. *Jonathan Livingston Seagull* is a novella. The allegory in the book is about a seagull named Jonathan Livingston who is different from the other seagulls. He is not content to simply survive, but yearns for something more. He wants to fly higher, faster and farther than any other seagull. Through his struggles, Jonathan discovers that true freedom and fulfillment come from being true to oneself, and that true success is not measured by material wealth or status, but by the quality of one's character and the joy of the journey. The book has been interpreted as a metaphor for the human search for meaning and purpose in life and serves as the perfect synopsis of what I am attempting to explore here, albeit with modern references and terminology. What I enhance upon, using Bach's metaphor, is how the religious influence of the American Story (Elder) has negatively impacted individual efforts to separate from the Flock and to discover for themselves, individually, what was just shared from above that true success is not measured by material wealth or status, but by the quality of one's character and the joy of the journey. After reading Bach's book the first time I was moved: I immediately 'got' the intended metaphor. I continued to re-read the book throughout my earlier adult years and the metaphor continued to reinforce my goal of achieving purpose not by material wealth or status, but rather by the pursuit of character and the joy of the journey (by collecting meaningful stories). A humorous aside here: I once lost my copy of JL, so I went to my nearest library to check out a copy but could not find it. I asked the librarian for help. We eventually found it cataloged in the children's holdings. I had to laugh, because here was a metaphor that even libraries didn't get, much less most of its intended audience: others who might have read it as self-help psychology. More evidence that it is what it is!

I subsequently found living for the 'joy of the journey' was my best option for becoming one:

> "... who has enjoyed the trust of pure women, the re-
> spect of intelligent men and the love of little children; who
> has filled his niche and accomplished his task; who has left

the world better than he found it, whether by an improved poppy, a perfect poem, or a rescued soul."

Living for the 'joy of the journey' is also why my storyline makes no reference to the need for the acquisition of 'material wealth or status'. I understood early on, living in the 'right' neighborhood, driving the 'right' cars, associating with the 'right' power people or pursuing a particular profession to maximize my earning potential was never going to address whatever level of 'emptiness' I might have felt along the way. I frequently wanted these things, but also accepted having these things was not going to automatically help or make me feel like I 'belonged'. These perks ultimately came to me in measured proportion, but not as sought-after goals, but rather as the fruits of my journey.

Mark Twain On America's Character:

It Is Now What It Was Then —Trumpism

Suite Judy Blue Eyes
Don't let the past remind us of what we are not now
(Crosby, Stills and Nash, 1969)

As previously acknowledged, Mark Twain dealt less with America's political factionalism and more with the Story of America's dual character. Twain's perspective on 1850-1900 American character significantly predates, yet exactly mirrors the seismic cultural shift back towards Red America's values we see happening today. His then-perspective becomes more predictive of today's American Character if one compares the similarities and differences between Twain's America and Trump's America. And, be assured, it is Trump's America! The balance alluded to by Twain below, has become significantly skewered towards Trumpism.

Twain, adept at telling any story, but especially America's 'Story' was also probably America's first great social psychologist; American Social Psychology did not really identify itself until post WW II years, according to Jonathan Haidt (*The Atlantic*, 2022). Social scientists have identified at least three major forces that collectively bind together successful democracies: social capital (extensive social networks with high levels of trust), strong institutions, and shared stories. Twain, erudite in his observations of the American Story spoke to all three in his writings and audience performances: Strong institutions (now significantly weakened by growing mistrust in religion, banks and especially the government)), social capital (torn asunder and lain bare with False Facts and rampant conspiracy theories on today's social media and now driving the American Culture Wars) and shared stories (A belief in the American Dream). It was through the shared story (now less equally shared and believed in) he spoke the truest!

> "On a chilly mid-November afternoon in 1869, a small man with a deranged mop of curly red hair and a wide-swept red mustache sauntered among the pedestrians in the 100 block of Tremont Street in Boston. He was desperately out of place with these men and women.

It was not just his clothing, black and drably functional, that marked this interloper. It was his gait, a curious
rocking shamble, conspicuously unurbane—the physical
equivalent of a hinterland drawl, which he also possessed.

He was headed to the publishing house of Ticknor and
Fields, … a prestigious publishing house whose authors,
many of whom lived nearby, commanded the first ranks
of America's emerging literature: Ralph Waldo Emerson;
Oliver Wendell Holmes; Nathaniel Hawthorne; Henry
Wadsworth Longfellow; Harriet Beecher Stowe; and Henry David Thoreau, among others.

The visitor's destination was … the tiny editorial office
of the Atlantic Monthly, where he was about to meet a
bookish fellow by the name of William Dean Howells.
Howells had written a favorable review of the visitor's
new book for the Atlantic's current issue." (Powers, *Mark
Twain, A Life*, 2005, p. 13-14).

By 1874, resultant of this initial meeting with Howells and the subsequent life-long friendship which resulted, the visitor became a major
contributor to the *Atlantic*. Powers' Prologue from *Mark Twain, A Life*
(2005) is surely the most accurate yet metaphorically-laden description
written to date which, in my mind, captures not only Twain during his
times, but subsequently Donald Trump, Trumpism and the MAGA
proponents who are genetically predisposed to yearn for a return to a
time which better matched their own unique perception of the American Story. What better way to describe Trumpism and everything it
represents than words like: "…small man, …deranged mop, …saun-
tered, …desperately out of place, …black and drably functional, …a
rocking shamble, …**conspicuously unurbane**, …(with an) hinterland drawl"?

Firstly, Power's physical description of Twain aptly serves as our
metaphor for the 1850-1900 proponents of American 'Trumpism'
which Twain chronicled, wrote about and spoke against. It also serves

as the appropriate metaphor for the Red America Trump would have us believe he fervently speaks to and for! For Twain's efforts in giving voice to their uniquely American literature, music, voices, politics, etc. Twain was tagged as 'the' representational figure of America in the last half of the 19th Century (Powers, *Mark Twain: A Life*, 2005, p. 17). It is in reality the descendants of these then-Trumpism-minded Americans who in their minds Made America Great the first time and whose descendants have handed Donald Trump the mantle as America's representational figure of today! The two (Twain and Trump) wore their mantles entirely differently and to entirely different ends. Trump frequently refers to this period of America for his inspiration for MAGA, but it is not to Twain's representational people he refers. No, Trump is referring to the Rockefellers, the Fords, Firestones, Mellon, Vanderbilts, Carnegies and other industrial giants and/or robber barons with whom Trump himself identifies, and to a time in which these industrialists ruled with an iron hand.

Twain, like Donald Trump, lived his life on the edges of self-control; he was quick to anger, hounded by guilt and anxiety, and subject to seismic shifts of mood. Equally withdrawn, irascible, given to pranks that could border on the mean spirited, yet not good at handling being pranked himself. He had the impulses of a rock star, often times berating audience members for some perceived slight (Powers, *Mark Twain: A Life*, 2005, p. 21).

Had we all been more like Mark Twain we might have been quicker to pick up on Twain's clues that Trumpism was coming; and not only was it coming but it wasn't going away anytime soon! Certainly not in our life time! He could not have known when it would get here, nor by what name it would be known, but Twain knew enough about the human character to understand the coming emergence and dominant manifestation of the darker side of America's character and story. A change he himself grew towards in his personal life in his later years.

"It is not a merit that it…(the human brain)…does the things which it is set to do——it can't HELP doing them." (Twain, *What is Man?*, 1906, p. 3)

If there is modern-day Mark Twain who can connect Twain's America to its modern-day cultural reality, then the best candidate would easily be George Saunders, a Mark Twain-style writer who has been acclaimed for saying it like it is, as Mark Twain did, and whose writing has been pegged by *Vanity Fair* as a 'shot in the arm for Americans, an antidote to the dumbing down virus plaguing our country'. George Saunders:

> "Huck and Tom represent two viable models of the American Character. They exist side by side in every American and every American action. America is, and always has been, undecided about whether it will be the United States of Tom or the United States of Huck. The United States of Tom looks at misery and says: Hey, I didn't do it. He looks at inequity and says: All my life I have busted my butt to get where I am, so don't come crying to me. Tom likes kings, codified nobility, **unquestioned privilege**. Huck likes people, fair play, spreading the truck around. Whereas Tom knows, Huck wonders. Whereas Huck hopes, Tom presumes. Whereas Huck cares, Tom **denies**. These two parts of the American Psyche have been at war since the beginning of the nation, ... and the hope of the nation ... is to embrace the Huck part and send the Tom part back up the river, where it belongs." (*The Braindead Megaphone*, 2007)

Besides Huck and Tom, what other evidence might we use to connect Twain's perspective to today's crises? How could Twain have known, one might ask? Why do we not know now?

> "A broad-minded man, who can see both sides of the question and is ready to hold two opposed truths while confessing that he cannot reconcile them, is at a manifest disadvantage with a narrow-minded man who sees but one side, sees it clearly, and is ready to interpret the whole Bible, or, if need be, the whole universe, in accordance with his formula. (H. Maynard Smith, Henry VIII and the Reformation, 1945)

The cold, hard, irrepressible truth about what drives Tom's views about unquestioned privilege, kings, nobility, presumptions and deniability is America's totally unique, in all the Westernized World, adherence to the religion which has shaped its Story! If one ever had the privilege of seeing Hal Holbrock perform *Mark Twain Tonight* live on either television or in person, one could not help but walk away from that experience with the gut-wrenching emotional impact with which Mark Twain, through Holbrook, felt our collective hypocrisy involving religion had ruined the American Character. Fast-forward 125 years post-Twain to today and **it is our hypocrisy, driven by our Religion, on all sides, which fuels our dichotomization of America beyond any ability to communicate with each other or to even reach any compromise!** It was our hypocrisy towards religion which Twain addressed most passionately! Twain was passionate in thinking the Ten Commandments left out the most important commandment of all: Man shall be indifferent to all other Religions, not tolerant of, but totally indifferent too. Twain saw the damage done everywhere in the name of Christianity (as in today's actions influencing abortion and LGBT+ rights), and addressed those issues in *Letters From Earth* (Bernard DeVoto, for Twain, 1962). While Americans are predisposed to be amoral, prudish and territorial it is the Far-Right Evangelical Movement which nurtured those traits to their fruition. Years from now historians will most certainly point to the Covid Pandemic as the breaking point for releasing generations of pent-up frustrations of the MAGA descendants. Prior to Covid Americans had assuredly, albeit begrudgingly, aligned themselves along the lines of temperament described by Twain:

> "But the law is the same. Where the temperament is two-thirds happy, or two-thirds unhappy, no political or religious beliefs can change the proportions. The vast majority of temperaments are pretty equally balanced; the intensities are absent, and this enables a nation to learn to accommodate itself to its political and religious circumstances ... and at last prefer them." (Twain, *What is Man?*, 1906)

Covid provided the opportunity for Red/Blue Extreme Americans, mostly Far-Right Evangelicals and the Politically Correct, Cancel Culture oriented Progressives to drop all semblance of decorum and to really show their truer character. Americans did not become mean-spirited during Covid, they merely allowed their mostly dormant mean-spirited temperaments to become more openly expressed. Like America's unique-to-America mass shooting rates and out-of-control gun rights issues, our reaction to Covid mandates was also unique-in-all-the-world-to-America. Only Americans could deny that the death rate for Covid was not unusual compared against the normal yearly death rate of Americans. Only Entitled Americans could get into fights on airplanes over others not wearing their masks. Only Americans could make a Constitutional issue out of even wearing face masks in public and in getting vaccinated!

Heartbreaking But True:

> Social media has witnessed and promulgated countless conspiracy theories regarding everything related to hot button issues with worrisome, detrimental effects, the worst of which led to this sharing from a Virginia mom whose son died in January of '23 and then she and many others whose children had died from the flu, but may or may not have been vaccinated with the COVID Vaccine had to endure attacks from the anti-vaxxers on FB and Twitter. The mother: "But vaccine opponents on the internet, who somehow assumed that a COVID shot was responsible for my son's death, thought my family's pain was funny. "Lol. Yay for the jab. Right? Right?" wrote one person on Twitter. "Your decision to vaccinate your son resulted in his death," wrote another. "This is all on YOU." "Murder in the first." (CNN)

America's reaction to Covid, was hallmark Trumpism and a classic example of how we are so very dependent upon our Negativity Bias and its manifested racism (tribalism) towards blacks, orientals, immigrants, outsiders, women, the LGBT+ community and to change of any kind.

Consider Mark Twain's own words:

> Man is a Reasoning Animal. Such is the claim. I think it is open to dispute. - "*The Lowest Animal*," 1897

Is this not how the Far-Right Evangelicals hostaged the Republican Party: That man is NOT a reasoning animal as Twain clearly suspected man was not? It has already been demonstrated that man is not as smart as he thinks he is nor has he evolved to a point where he is as smart as he needs to be to consistently strive to achieve the Greater Good, with humanity, morality, integrity, meaning and purpose? (Self, *I Think, Therefore I Am … probably wrong*, 2020). Again is this not how Red America totally cowered to Trump, especially in light of the fact that Trump has never had a guiding philosophy for Republicans to espouse? Most predictive of Twain's understanding of what would eventually happen to the Republican Party, in the name of Trumpism:

> "Nations do not THINK, they only FEEL. They get their feelings at secondhand through their temperaments, not their brains. A nation can be brought—by force of circumstances, not argument—to reconcile itself to ANY KIND OF GOVERNMENT OR RELIGION THAT CAN BE DEVISED; in time it will fit itself to the required conditions; later, it will prefer them and will fiercely fight for them. …All of history is full of … every kind of government that can be thought of, … each nation KNOWING it has the only true religion and the only sane system of government, each despising all the others, each an ass and not suspecting it, each proud of its fancied supremacy, each perfectly sure it is the pet of God, …(Mark Twain, *What Is Man*, 1906, p. 60)

Not only did Twain accurately capture America's malaise of character, tainted by its religion, but he also understood its evolutionary predisposition to devolve. He recognized early on that man made decisions quickly and emotionally; not methodically and rationally. We have the benefit of modern-day neuroscience to help us better understand how we make the decisions we do. The influence modernism had on Twain is visible in all of his writings. One such modernist, Charles Darwin, had a great impact on Twain. Twain was very familiar with the writings of Darwin as he owned thirteen of his books. He also had a deep admiration for Darwin's work and often referenced it within his own writings. The majority of his references to Darwin are positive, and become even more favorable as his literary career progressed. It was through Twain's acceptance of the Darwinian theory of evolution that his skepticism toward Christianity began to grow, leading to his lack of understanding as to why anyone would accept the Bible as literal.

As true pioneers involved in nation building Americans have always maximized their genetic predisposition to the survival of the fittest. We perceive ourselves as the world's ultimate warriors. We are predisposed to react, not think. We are so full of our own individual and collective self-importance that we have never really had the desire nor, owing to Twain's 'the brain is a machine and nothing more' analogy, to pause, step back and take a serious look at the absurdity of our self-made crises; real or hypothetical! We are so caught up in the immediacy and urgency of our perceived slights we are unable to heed the lessons of previous generations to realize the seeds of our crises were set long ago.

We are nothing but echoes. We have no thoughts of our own, no opinions of our own, we are but a compost heap made up of the decayed heredities, moral and physical. (Mark Twain's *Notebook*, 1933)

In the last decades of his life, Twain, like F. Scott Fitzgerald and Earnest Hemingway after him, was forced to accept the inevitable chaotic cruelty of the world, and grew increasingly disappointed with his fellow human beings for a broad range of reasons: -cupidity (lust for wealth), greed, hypocrisy, arrogance, pride, etc.. This change was most evident in two works he finished just before his death and both of which were subsequently published posthumously, and quickly forgotten: *Letters from Earth* (1962) and *What is Man?* (1906). Letters focused on Twain's views on the deleterious effects of Religion and the Bible on Man's character, while *What is Man?* best reflected Darwin's influence on Twain's thoughts about the evolutionary nature of Man's character and Man's inability to change his responses, beliefs, and ideologies; views which hold especially true in today's crisis of American character.

As well as his views on religion it is Twain's assessment of man's character which has so much application to today's firestorms. In Twain's posthumously published short story, *What is Man?* (1906), he assumes the role of both conversants: an Old Man (wizened) and the Young Man (naive) who have been dialoguing. "The Old Man had asserted that the human being is merely a machine, and nothing more. ...(Sayest)... the Old Man: as soon as a Truth-Seeker finds what he is thoroughly convinced is the Truth, he seeks no further, but gives the rest of his days to hunting junk to patch it and caulk it and prop it with, and make it weather-proof and keep it from caving in on him". (How prophetic were both Maynard Smith's and F. Scott Fitzgerald's observations about one's inability to hold two counter-intuitive thoughts in one's head at one time in explaining today's Trumpist protagonists!) Twain's Old Man clearly anticipated this would be the mechanism by which 'Trumpists' would attempt to rationalize the 'Big Steal", or prevent meaningful gun control or to deny women control over their own bodies!

Continues Twain's Old Man:

> "This is the law, keep it in your mind. From the cradle to his grave a man never does a single thing which has any first and foremost object but one—to secure peace of mind, spiritual comfort, for **himself**: ... Man's sole impulse...(is)...the securing of his own approval. ... Man the machine—the impersonal engine. Whatsoever a man is, is due to his make and to the influences brought to bear upon it by his heredities, his habitat, his associations."

As the Old Man and the Young Man continue dissecting Man's Nature they remind us again that **we are predisposed to act and behave in predetermined ways**. Most of us, most of the time, make decisions and engage in actions programmed into our 'hunter' and 'nester' genes which have evolved and operated over eons of generations. Our very survival depends on our instinctually reacting to the events in our environment. Decisions which were(are) emotionally driven, hyper-reactive, and often morally illogical come from way down deep in our limbic system. The limbic system is a collective term for brain structures that are involved in processing emotions. It is also **responsible for all human behavior, all decision-making; it allows the possibility of making living beings act smartly without having to think smartly!** On top of that the limbic system processes information 200 times faster than the cognitive brain! Yet, it is the cognitive brain, driven by the Anterior Cingulate Cortex (ACC), upon which we rely to make proactive, rational decisions. Proactive moral judgements are made resultant of rational thinking, not emotional reactions.

"—but YOU did not create the materials out of which …(man)… is formed. They are odds and ends of thoughts, impressions, feelings, gathered unconsciously from a thousand books, a thousand conversations, and from streams of thought and feeling which have flowed down into your heart and brain out of the hearts and brains of centuries of ancestors. PERSONALLY you did not create even the smallest microscopic fragment of the materials out of which your opinion is made; and personally you cannot claim even the slender merit of PUTTING THE BORROWED MATERIALS TOGETHER. That was done AUTOMATICALLY—by your mental machinery, in strict accordance with the law of that machinery's construction. And you not only did not make that machinery yourself, but you have **NOT EVEN ANY COMMAND OVER IT.**" (Twain, *What is Man?*, 1906, P.4).

"The act must do HIM good, FIRST; otherwise he will not do it. He may THINK he is doing it solely for the other person's sake, but it is not so; he is contenting his own spirit first—the other person's benefit has to always take SECOND place." P.16

"Then perhaps there is something that he loves MORE than he loves peace—THE APPROVAL OF HIS NEIGH-BORS AND THE PUBLIC. And perhaps there is something which he dreads more than he dreads pain—the DISAPPROVAL of his neighbors and the public. If he is sensitive to shame he will go to the field—not because his spirit will be ENTIRELY comfortable there, but because it will be more comfortable there than it would be if he remained at home." p.19

"You remember that you said that I said training was EVERYTHING. I corrected you, and said "training and ANOTHER thing." That other thing is TEMPERA-MENT—that is, the disposition you were born with. YOU CAN'T ERADICATE YOUR DISPOSITION" p.62

As did Mark Twain, I truly believe in the existence and reality of the Story. We come into the world alone and we go out of the world alone and what we do in between is our Story. Since our primary purpose for existing is procreation and mastering the hunt and nesting, what becomes our individual purpose when we fulfill the larger purpose? The almost overwhelming challenge though is we come into the world with our story mostly written through our predispositions and genetics, and we simply follow along; as are doing the millions of Americans who exist in denial of such reality. They are born, and mindlessly live out their programming to be inculcated by their parents, or not, become trained, or not, get married, or not, have children, or not, contribute to the larger society, or not and eventually die alone.

What does exist, though beat down, is personal integrity and proactive morality. Twain's unique perspective was he did realize the importance of The Story over Religion. The hypocrisy of Religion was a common theme in his speeches and writing. He spoke to the fact that America was moving away from personal integrity and proactive morality (if it had ever even had it)! He became the antagonist to those who purveyed 'Trumpism' as the American Story. He seems to have accepted Madison's view that as long as factions remained in equivalent numerical balance societies could survive. As Haidt has pointed out, for at least the past ten years our Story has precipitously grown out of balance. In reality, it probably became precipitously unbalanced about the time Ronald Reagan became President. Our integrity and morality are being consumed by Negativity Bias, exasperating our cultural death spiral and Mark Twain saw it and spoke to it!.

Twain: "It is curious that physical courage should be so common in the world and moral courage so rare!"

Twain: "The moral sense enables one to perceive morality, and avoid it. The immoral sense enables one to perceive immorality and enjoy it."

Twain: "We are incapable of choosing when to behave morally or not.

What Is The American Story

America's 'Story' has always been about democracy as an experiment; an experiment dominated by mostly white hunter/nesters. It is an experiment in the viability of the marriage of the two opposing and yet behaviorally predisposed Tribes which settled America.

America isn't easy (and never has been):

"America is advanced citizenship. You got to want it bad. ...(and the religious far right) ...isn't the least bit interested in solving ... (America's cultural issues). They... are interested in two things, and two things only: making you afraid of it, and telling you who is to blame for it. That ladies and gentlemen is how you win elections...we have serious problems to solve and we need serious people to solve them. (Michael Douglas as President Andrew Shepherd, *The American President*, 1995).

Mitt Romney, retiring US Senator on the rot in the GOP base:

"A very large portion of my party, really doesn't believe in the Constitution." He'd realized this only recently, he said. America was only a few months removed from an attempted coup instigated by Republican leaders, and Romney was wrestling with some difficult questions.

Was the authoritarian element of the GOP a product of President Trump, or had it always been there, just waiting to be activated by a sufficiently shameless demagogue? And what role had the members of the mainstream establishment—people like him, the reasonable Republicans—played in allowing the rot on the right to fester?' (Tom Nichols, *The Atlantic Daily, When Americans Abandon the Constitution*, Sept. 23, 2023)

The very best book I never read was "*What You Think Of Me Is None of My Business*", by the Reverend Teri Cole-Whittaker. Didn't have to read it because the title said it all! And while I did actually read the book as well as the following articles, I really did not need to because, once again, the titles say it all! Time and again history shows anyone who might be looking that all great societies eventually succumb to their own, internal cultural death spirals. First tier societies become second tier societies. 'It's been clear for quite a while now that Red America and Blue America are becoming like two different countries claiming the same territory, with two different versions of the Constitution, economics, and American history', (Haidt, *Atlantic*, 2022). Burns (From Lang, below): "This is a simple choice between Bedford Falls and Pottersville: Where does America want to live?" The disturbing irony is that both Red America and Blue America would passionately argue that they are defending Bedford Falls. They would both be wrong!

"Why The Past Ten Years of American Life Have Been Uniquely Stupid, …It's not just a phase", Jonathan Haidt, *The Atlantic*, May 2022.

"Are the Last Rational Republicans in Denial? The current **GOP is beyond rescue**", Tom Nichols, *Atlantic Daily*, July 6, 2022 …[**As**, in truth, **is the Democratic Party**]…

"This Is How America's Culture War Death Spirals. Why Disney vs. DeSantis is the Future of Politics", Derek Thompson, *The Atlantic*, May 22, 2022

"Opinion: Why do smart Republicans say stupid things?", Dana Milbank, *The Washington Post,* March 28, 2022

"Ken Burns' Urgent Warning: Why He's **Scared for America's Future**", Brent Lang, *Variety*, Feb. 16, 2022.

Today's negative narrative of the American Story is not about the death of American Politics or America's form of government. The American Story is about the inevitable death of the American marriage! American politics will endure in some form or fashion. While America may have started out as a Democratic Republic with a strong element of oligarchy and a weak element of democracy that is no longer the case. Today America is a de facto plutocracy with a weak democratic facade. Herein the death of the American Story is really about the downward spiral of America's attempted marriage of character! And since marriage is nothing without commitment, compromise and character, factors currently lacking in today's cultural America, our national 'story' is clearly in decline!

Ever notice that in our own relationships with a significant-other spouse or partner, how exasperating simple conversations can become? Two people, supposedly compatible and into each other enough to willingly enter into a serious relationship or even marriage can be having a conversation with each other, using the very same words, and neither one has a clue what the other one is talking about, and further, can not even fathom how and why their partner can think and say the things coming out of their mouth? This is exactly what is happening in America between Red and Blue America. Well, that's marriage!

Nation building is very much like building a successful marriage. Success in both requires meaningful two-way conversation and compromise. Marriages typically work best when in the beginning both spouses are able to move far away from well intentioned yet interfering family and friends with the pressures they add to building a compatible marriage. Too often when newly weds disagree they will immediately rely on family and/or friends to support their point of view, rather than make the effort to work through the issue towards compromise. Yet when newly-weds can move away from their support systems they are much more likely to make the additional effort to resolve issues between themselves rather than give up or run to others for support. The analogy applies to nation building. In the beginning of the American experiment the relative numbers in each pool of Red/Blue America were proportionally small with each group having moved very far away from their home countries and support bases. Red and Blue America were forced to develop mutually beneficial solutions, i.e., compromise. In today's America compromise between Red and Blue America is quickly becoming DOA and both sides verbalize as much in every public comment they make about the other side. Keep in mind the failure rate for marriages traditionally runs around 50%, so is it really all that challenging to think America's Story has a 50-50 chance of survival?

So why do marriages fail? Typically both sides are incompatible. Moving from 'me' to 'us' successfully requires compatibility and then compromise. The best marriages are never perfect. Marriage requires giving up individuality to some extent for the Greater Good of the marriage. It especially requires trust. Each side has to be able to listen to the other and not only listen, but truly hear and build a sense of trust in each other that workable solutions can be found. It is often said that in marriage opposites attract, but do those marriages really work? Although over 80% of people believe opposites attract, its not necessarily true. It is not opposites which attract us but certain complementary personality traits. A 2013 study by Eharmony confirmed these conclusions: opposites may attract, but its the similarities which tend to carry the day in successful relationships and stories. Common values and ethics are the common denominator in stories of happy marriages and successful nation building. So am I discussing marriage or nation building here? Is there a difference? The facts tend to play in my favor that they are not so different, and Red/Blue Extreme America and Red/Blue Moderate America never truly shared common values nor a common ethic.

Red/Blue Extreme America and Red/Blue Moderate America could not be more incompatible, and the fact that over 335,000,000 of them now populate a confined space and each has unlimited access to conspiracy theories, fake facts, opinions and family/friend support when arguing with each other, we will probably never be more together than we aren't today.

A house divided against itself cannot stand.
(Abraham Lincoln, June, 1858)

… and yet one-hundred and sixty-five years later congresswoman **Marjorie Taylor Greene** (R-Ga). can call for the U.S. to be separated into Red and Blue states and has the sufficient audience for it to be taken seriously; "**We need a national divorce. We need to separate by red states and blue states and shrink the federal government,**" Green isn't the first Republican to call for some form of secession, and there are indications that support for secession has been growing since the 2020 elections. A June 2021 poll by *Bright Line Watch* and YouGov found that 66% of Southern Republicans supported leaving the U.S. and forming a new country. Support was also high among Democrats in the West, where 47% supported a division.

The American Story has had many chapter headings. There are several on Nation Building; a couple on Identity Formation and several more on the American Dream, but not so many warning how the American marriage could implode on itself and the probable lasting effect of that implosion. The catalyst for those chapters on implosion was written long ago, but the acceleration of its implosion is a more recent phenomenon (during the past 40 years and especially during the last 15 years!) and is still being written. **To reiterate though, the social-psychological function of story is to build identity, hence the purpose of the American Story is to articulate, inculcate, and reinforce the values and beliefs of those born into or seeking membership into the American Tribe to assure America's culture remains true to itself for inter-and-intra-generational conformity** (To assure conformity is a hint of the origin of the catalyst for its demise). Stories give us our sense of identity in, and belonging to, something larger than ourselves. Stories define our membership in and the expectations for us by 'our' Tribe. In theory stories motivate our move away from infantile narcissism towards a healthy assimilation into someone capable of contributing to the Greater Good. Stories serve as morality plays to teach moral lessons about abstract concepts like truth, goodness, honesty, equality and liberty, among others. Remember Harari (*Sapiens*, 2014): "When we look for the meaning of life, we want a story that will explain what reality is all about and what my particular role is in the cosmic drama"?

And still, as Twain also observed, Americans have always been, at heart, good people. Consistently charitable, the first to pitch in during natural disasters, willing to assist and feed neighbors during familial dark times, etc., just afraid or unwilling to speak up in the face of injustice to others. Since it truly seems 'Like Attracts Like', and that Story promotes conformity and sameness with little tolerance for allowing deviation from story then charity is only available to those who are *primarily of our 'like' (Tribe)*! From its inception the American Story has only been available to Red America(n) Men! Why else would we be unsuccessfully addressing rampant racism, immigration issues, glass ceilings for women, abortion rights, LGBT+ rights or why else would the Far-right Evangelicals contend the Bible excludes women from being pastors in the Baptist church?

Stories, like marriages, most-assuredly have a downside. Since they are about preservation of the species, survival of the fittest and continuation of 'our' Tribe, they also connote an element of Negativity Bias and discrimination in assimilating members. 'Like Attracts Like', so story promotes conformity and sameness, with little tolerance for allowing deviation from story. Stories implicitly address two points: one, how one's own Tribe's values are better than our own individual values, and two, how our Tribe's values are better than another Tribe's values, e.g, Religion and life-style choices. Mark Twain spoke directly to this point regarding religion when he said: "Man shall be indifferent to all other religions, not tolerant of, but totally indifferent to'. The very need for 'conformity' in story to define one's purpose automatically implies/conveys a deeper, darker side to story, and America's Story has clearly shifted to prioritizing its darker side in an effort to regain, in its own mind at least, an earlier, simpler and less confusing image of itself. Americans have a morbid curiosity and attraction to the horror story genre as entertainment, e.g., the immense popularity of *Fargo* or the *American Horror Story*. But is it entertainment or a subconsciously acceptable acknowledgement of the existence of our 'hunter' genes and the biology behind our beliefs in the Devil and all things evil which we engage in to scare us into adopting our Tribes's larger story? A favorite MAGA tactic used by the far-right to embarrass non-MAGA believers for not being true believers in the American Story is to loudly and belligerently challenge them with 'Aren't you a Patriot?'. Who's going to say no to that question? Being a Patriot is a major part of belonging to the larger American story (Remember, I still get teary-eyed at the playing of the National Anthem and I want to continue to get emotional each time I hear it, because I have hinged my "I am a Patriot' card on belonging to the American Way of life!). If I say no, then I am clearly not American and MAGA has justified its Self-Righteousness to itself! It is only too easy to conclude this need to affirm membership in tribe originates in our biology and provides legitimacy to the existence of Negativity Bias and negative narratives in Story.

The American Story began as hope, a vision, an ideal, but mostly only white men could participate in the story! It was freedom from religious persecution, and the opportunity for un-bounded individualism and financial independence. Life, liberty and the pursuit of happiness presented opportunities for a country which did evolve to be larger than life, do things on a bigger scale, to be industrially innovative, and a country with a can-do attitude! America's identity became inseparable from that of a Superman. America was Superman. The ideation of Superman seems to best summarize the evolution of the American Story. By 1942 America and Superman both became synonymous for:

Truth, Justice and the American Way

So what is/was the American Way? Why, ...

**Baseball, hot dogs, and apple pie, or
Baseball, hot dogs, apple pie and
Chevrolet on the Fourth of July,
or
Motherhood and apple pie**

... of course!

America's Story has wrapped itself around a plethora of cliche's of American idioms which represent our core beliefs, wholesomeness, traditions, most cherished values and most deeply engrained characteristics. Americans and the World came to identify these slogans as the 'American Way', and the very basis of America's **Identity**

The American Story is supposedly about the attainability of the **American Dream**: The ideal by which equality of opportunity is available to anyone, allowing for one's highest aspirations and goals to be able to be achieved, if only one was willing to work hard, sacrifice and endure. The concept is so engrained in the world culture it has its own definition in the Oxford Dictionary:

> 'The ideal that every citizen of America should have an equal opportunity to achieve success and prosperity through hard work, determination and initiative'

And yet:

Ellen Swallow Richards

… Graduated Westward Academy, second oldest high school in Massachusetts, 1862

… Graduated Vassar College, B.A., 1870

… Becomes the first woman ever admitted to M.I.T., after a special vote by the Faculty of the Institute, 1870, although M.I.T. made it clear "her admission did not establish a precedent for the general admission of females".

… Graduated M.I.T., with a B.S. degree, as the first woman in America to ever earn a degree in Chemistry, 1873. The B.S. should have been an M.A., but M.I.T. would not allow its first advanced degree to be awarded to a female so denied her M.A. giving her a B.A. instead. M.I.T. did not actually award any advanced degrees until 1886.

Hidden Figures

The 2016 movie and book Hidden Figures, brought to light the many contributions of black women to astrophysics. The book highlights the experiences of three specific black women: Katherine Johnson, Dorothy Vaughan, and Mary Jackson. These women lived the phenomenal true story of black female mathematicians at NASA, who were on the leading edge of the feminist and civil rights movement--a powerful, revelatory contribution that is as essential to our understanding of race, discrimination, and achievement in modern America as any story could be.

The Tulsa Black Wall Street Massacre

A white racist massacre that took place between May 31 and June 1, 1921. Mobs of white residents, some of whom had been appointed as deputies and armed by city government officials, attacked black residents and destroyed homes and businesses of the Greenwood District in Tulsa, OK. The event is considered one of the worst incidents of racial violence in American history. The attackers burned and destroyed more than 35 square blocks of the neighborhood—at the time one of the wealthiest black communities in the United States. More than 800 people were admitted to hospitals, and as many as 6,000 black residents of Tulsa were interned in large facilities, many of them for several days. The Oklahoma Bureau of Vital Statistics officially recorded 36 dead.

Trail Of Tears

Between 1816 and 1840, tribes located between the original states and the Mississippi River, including Cherokees, Chickasaws, Choctaws, Creeks, and Seminoles, signed more than 40 treaties ceding their lands to the U.S. In his 1829 inaugural address, President Andrew Jackson set a policy to relocate eastern Indians. In 1830 it was endorsed, when Congress passed the Indian Removal Act to force those remaining to move west of the Mississippi. Between 1830 and 1850, about 100,000 American Indians living between Michigan, Louisiana, and Florida moved west after the U.S. government coerced treaties or used the U.S. Army against those resisting. Many were treated brutally. An estimated 3,500 Creeks died in Alabama and on their westward journey. Some were transported in chains.

Japanese-Americans Placed in Internment Camps

Within two months of the Japanese attack on Pearl Harbor, in an effort to curb potential Japanese espionage, President Franklin D. Roosevelt issued Executive Order 9066 which approved the relocation of Japanese-Americans into internment camps. The executive order paved the way for forced relocation of Japanese-Americans living on the west coast. During the six months following the issue of EO 9066, over 100,000 Japanese-Americans found themselves placed into concentration camps within the United States. These concentration camps were called "relocation camps." This order stayed in place until President Harry S. Truman signed Executive Order 9742 on June 25, 1946. This allowed Japanese-Americans to return to their homes. Many of the newly released Japanese-Americans returned home to find their belongings stolen or their property sold. Japanese-Americans who were returning home faced discrimination and prejudice from the civilian population.

US Government Turns Away Thousands
Of Jewish Refugees, Fearing They Were Spies

'In a long tradition of 'persecuting the refugee', the State Department and FDR claimed that Jewish immigrants could threaten national security. WWII prompted the largest displacement of human beings the world has seen—although today's refugee crisis is starting to approach its unprecedented scale. With millions of European Jews displaced from their homes the US had a poor track record offering asylum'. (Daniel Gross, *Smithsonian Magazine*, Nov. 18, 2015)

US Department of the Interior Releases Report:
Federal Indian Boarding School Initiative Investigative Report
May, 2022

The *Yellowstone* prequel spinoff *1923* features a shocking depiction of forced assimilation programs initiated by western settlers and Christian missionaries against Indigenous American and First Nations Canadian children; children who were forcibly removed from their homes during the ages of 4-16 and forced to become 'Anglicised'.

The portrayal of the abuses in *1923* was authentic and based on preliminary findings of an investigation of Canadian residential schools for First Nations Children. The Canadian investigation prompted similar investigations in America after Canadian investigators discovered 215 native children remains at the Kamloop Residential School in Canada in May 2021. In Canada over 17,000 indigenous children attended 80 residential schools and received similar treatment as their American counterparts.

Interior Secretary Deb Haaland held back tears as she described the scope of the investigation that identified 408 federal Indian boarding schools across 37 states that operated between 1819 and 1969. New Mexico had at least 43 of these schools, the third most in the country behind Oklahoma (76) and Arizona (47).

In the late 19th century, the government forced families to send their children to these church-operated schools where they were brainwashed into viewing their own culture as inferior to that of the one brought by Western settlers. Forced to embrace English as the only mode of communication, they were punished if they even uttered so much as a word in their native tongue. In the beginning, only a couple of these institutions were in operation, including the Fort Shaw Indian School in Montana. It wasn't long, however, before almost 200 more sprang up across the United States, with most of them operating in states like Oklahoma, Minnesota, and South Dakota. Many of these children experienced abuse, sexual assault, and punishment at the hands of the residential staff and were converted to various Christian religions. Hundreds of Indigenous children were killed at these schools and those that survived were never the same. Of the over 50 (53 to date and still growing) burial sites discovered, over 500 bodies have been located, though not exhumed to respect Indian after-life beliefs. One of the most well-known boarding schools of the late 1800s was the Carlisle Indian School in Carlisle, Pennsylvania where the children of Geronimo's Apache tribe were sent while Geronimo and his remnant tribe were sent to Florida and remained. With the goal of complete assimilation, the infamous motto of Colonel Richard Henry Pratt, headmaster of the school for 25 years, was "Kill the Indian, save the man." (Maka Monture Paka, *American Genocide: the Crimes of National American Boarding Schools*, Vanity Fair podcast, May 2023)

January 6, 2021 US Insurrection

Five people died either shortly before, during, or following the event. One was shot by Capital Police, another died of a drug overdose, and three died of natural causes, including a police officer. Many people were injured, including 138 police officers. Four officers who responded to the attack died by suicide within seven months. As of July 7, 2022, monetary damages caused by attackers exceed $2.7 million. Over 1,400 participants were eventually convicted of assault, entering restricted government property, destruction of government property, theft of government property, and conspiracy, among others. Called to action by Trump, thousands of his supporters gathered in Washington, D.C., on January 5 and 6 to support his false claim that the 2020 election had been "stolen by emboldened radical-left Democrats and to demand that Vice President Mike Pence and Congress reject Biden's victory. Starting at noon on January 6, at a "Save America" rally on the Ellipse, Trump gave a speech in which he repeated false claims of election irregularities, and though he encouraged his supporters to march to the Capitol to peacefully make their voices heard, he said, "If you don't fight like hell, you're not going to have a country anymore". During and after his speech, thousands of attendees, some armed, walked to the Capitol, and hundreds breached police perimeters as Congress was beginning the electoral vote count.

The American Story Originates as Nation Building

The Declaration of Independence espouses a country which supports, promotes and embodies the pursuit of ideals like "Life, Liberty and the Pursuit of Happiness". Freedom of speech, religious freedom, protection of human rights, individualism, and capitalism became the foundational pillars of a newly forming Nation.

Nation building inspired and supported stories about exploring and settling new frontiers; stories about manufacturing prowess, industrial innovations and inventions; stories about coming together to help each other and the World in times of need and disasters. As America grew, its story was evermore becoming the story of the 'American Way'; a story of rich pride and opportunity and individual and national success. But at what cost?

The Beginning Was The End:

The Declaration of Independence was certainly written to be America's last chapter. It has not turned out as envisioned. Written in 1776 it has become a chapter now hurtling, not as intended, but rather to its own demise. The American Story or Dream, as intended was 'written and lived' around these words:

> "We hold these truths to be self-evident, that all men are created equal, that they are endowed by their Creator with certain unalienable Rights, that among these are Life, Liberty and the pursuit of Happiness"

…and which were eventually expanded and placed on a tablet at the feet of the Statue of Liberty:

> "Give me your tired, your poor,
> Your huddled masses yearning to breathe free,
> The wretched refuse of your teeming shore.
> Send these, the homeless, tempest-tost to me,
> I lift my lamp beside the golden door!"
> (Emma Lazarus)

...but now on that same tablet, invisible to the naked eye its post-script continues as:

.…... unless, of course, you're black, yellow,
Hispanic, Gay, Lesbian, Jew, Muslim, Non-Baptist, Homeless, Liberal, Conservative or elect to have an abortion!

...or these could be the new post-script:

Give me your tired, your poor…
But not too tired, not too poor.
And we will give you the red tape,
… and the looks, the stares that say you are not
where or what you should be, not quite, not yet,
you will never live up to us.
(Naomi Shihab Nye, in *Denied, Detained Deported*,
by Ann Bausem, 2019)

… or these:

Give us your tired, your poor, or Don't
(Edward O'Donnell, NY Times, 2006)

Trump vs Biden, 2020?:

"The presidential contest between an embattled incumbent seeking reelection in a bitterly divided country and his well-known challenger dominated the national spotlight. The hard-fought campaign featured vicious attacks in partisan newspapers. The challenger's supporters accused the president of authoritarian impulses, bullying his subordinates, trampling constitutional rights, and destroying foreign alliances. The president's allies fired back. They claimed their opponent was an atheist bent on seizing Bibles from the homes of American Christians, and they whispered tales of animal sacrifices and sexual transgressions by the president's adversary. The challenger's supporters anxiously worried that the incumbent would seek to hold on to power even in defeat. The president's supporters believed the republic's survival was at stake should their opponent occupy the Executive Mansion." (Ray Tyler, *The Sedition Act of 1798,* July, 2016, MAHG Graduate)

The above election occurred in 1800 and featured a struggle between John Adams and Thomas Jefferson. Jefferson triumphed, in part, because Adams signed the infamous Sedition Act of 1798. This act made it a crime for anyone to "write, print, utter, or publish ... false, scandalous, and malicious writing or writings against the government of the United States, the Congress, or the President.

The Southern Cross
So we cheated and we lied and we tested,
And we never failed to fail it was the easiest
thing to do. You will survive being vested
...'Cause the truth you might be runnin'
from is so small, But it's as big as the
promise, the promise of a comin' day
(Steven Stills of CSN, 1971)

So What Happened To The American Way? ...

... it was, and remains to this day an illusion! An illusion knowingly and equally, unknowingly, promoted and participated in every single day by each and everyone of us. We want to believe in Truth, Justice and the American Way. We need for the American Story, OUR story, to be a story of unity, integrity, purpose and meaning. But it remains an unattainable illusion none-the-less. Certainly an illusion when it comes to our unity. America is not united nor has it ever been. We are the **United** States of America in name only!

Inspired by its highly successful *"I'd like to Teach the World to Sing (In Perfect Harmony)"* campaign in 1971 to promote world-market unity, *Coca Cola,* after 9/11 and again in the wake of the George Floyd/Black Lives Matter demonstrations, floated a new unity slogan:

We Live As Many, We Stand As One

I liked it. I thought it very accurately captured the prevailing public reaction and subsequent response to both 9/11 and Black Lives Matter! The slogan flopped! American unity of purpose may have been truish during WWII and certainly after 9/11, but little evidence persists for other examples of America standing as one. For reasons never publicly detailed, except possibly in advertising/marketing 'how-not-to' seminars, Coke took such flack for trying to promote unity, the ads only ran once or twice before being pulled back, both times!

… and still the illusion continues. If we were really interested in the American Way as a positive unity of purpose we would devote more of our time and energy comparing our view of ourselves (what we *espouse* as the American Way) against the view the rest of the World (and in-truth, the view half of America holds) holds about us (the *in-use, or actual* perception). Is the way we think we are a match for how the rest of the World sees us? (Argyris & Schon, *Theory Into Practice, Increasing Professional Effectiveness,* 1974)

Argyris concerned himself with measuring the amount of agreement between our *espoused* and *in-use viewpoints* regarding personal and institutional effectiveness. How we think we project ourselves and how others actually see us provides a statistical measure of Congruence. The more closely aligned the two views are the more 'Congruent' they can be said to be and the more healthy our institutions, personal values and perceptions and actions are. There can be no doubt America is excessively in-congruent: our view of who we are is illusionary and totally out of sync with our own story and lacks congruence with the more equalitarian view upon which the American Story was supposedly created and with which the rest of the world and at least half of America views their own Story.

There is no questioning America is the most powerful nation on Earth, but where does its respect monitor reside? Does our power emanate from being the purveyor of truth, justice and the American Way?

Or, does our power now partially come from our dominating military power which we wield as a part of our Teddy Roosevelt inspired 'speak softly and carry a big stick: you will go far' worldwide diplomacy? Truth, Justice and the American Way has yielded to False Facts, outright Lies, Justice for some, and the Military-Industrial Complex. Our power mostly comes from the almighty dollar. The dollar is our Religion! We have the world's strongest economy which we use to wield The American Way but not for truth and justice. The American Way has clearly become the pursuit of the dollar as the carrot, backed by our military as the big stick? When Trump utters MAGA, he is personally referring to the 1880-1920s when the American Industrial Revolution was being orchestrated by the wealthy, without regulation and without consideration for the little man and the effects their actions had on the individual rights of others. Trumps continues to visualize himself in the company of hard-fisted capitalists like the Rockefellers, Mellons, Carnegies, Goulds, Vanderbilts, Firestones, Macys, Fords, Fisks, McCormicks, Flaglers, Pullmans, Stanfords, Astors, J.P. Morgans, Fricks, Schwabs, etc.

Rich in natural resources, wealthy beyond compare, the shopping mall of the world, the most envied nation for its life style and the most visited nation. But again is it our pursuit of a greed-driven American Dream or our Story of truth, justice, baseball, hot dogs and apple pie which we want reflected in how we live the American Way? Looking in from the outside it seems to me that others would conclude we have become indifferent regarding our Story's foundation of self-respect and identity! Somewhere along the way **The American Way** became recognized more as a caricature of the **Ugly American**, at home and abroad! The *Ugly American* (Burdick, E., & Lederer, W., 1958) was written to depict the failures of the US diplomatic corp in Southeast Asia, but, like baseball, hot dogs and apple pie… over time *The Ugly American* became another American idiom depicting Americans as "loud and ostentatious, who isolate themselves socially (…within the confines of its military might, the Christian Bible and far-right evangelicalism…) and who live pretentiously." Even today when Americans visit overseas the enduring impressions we leave are of a people who are loud, arrogant, rude, discourteous, ill-mannered, angry, etc.

As previously mentioned the foundation of America's Nation Building was pillared on religious freedom, individualism, and capitalism. Over time those pillars have morphed into 1.) a majorative religion predominated by fractured right-wing-Evangelicalism, 2.) individualism which has devolved into entitlement and anger, and 3.) capitalism driven by individual and corporate greed. That is our current reality. That is our American Story. That is our current American Way and American Dream!

With regards to Religious Freedom, we know that in America today, and as far back as Mark Twain's own recorded observations, religious freedom really means 'without tolerance' for other religions, which includes 'without tolerance' for the poor, the LGBT+ community, women's reproductive rights, voting and leadership rights, ethnic diversity, immigrants, etc.. The freedom of religion leg in America, with its tumultuous past, has lead to a multitude of denominations, but none as loud nor which has contributed more to the American Malaise than the far-right Evangelicals, who to this day fight each other, and are clearly driving the culture wars in America.

If there is One God how can there be so many American Christian denominations which believe, based on their human interpretation of the One Bible, that their God is the One True God? Modern Orthodox Judaism which originated somewhere around 1818-1821 is still fundamentally one interpretation of the much older Orthodox Judaism. The Catholic bibles have not varied since the original canon was approved at the Council of Hippo in 397 AD. Muslims believe that Gabriel brought the word of God to Muhammad verbatim and the Quran was divinely protected from any alteration or change. Even the roots of Buddhism lie in the religious thought of Iron Age India from around the middle of the first millennium BCE. All, except for the Christian Bible continue to provide relevant, consistent Story which yields, for those true believers anyway, their version of integrity, meaning and purpose even if mistaken and misguided in their view of espousing the Greater Good and positive Morality. Their stories have remained constant.

However, from the very beginning religion in America fell into the hands of 16th century, Martin Luther Anglo-Saxon Protestants, (today's Far-Right Evangelicals) even though only 1 in 5 settlers affiliated with church. Today, as then, it has been the minority Anglo/Saxon Evangelicals who came to forge national identity, all-the-while supporting only a narrow slice of America, never acknowledging the new nation's racism, hedonism, violence, conformism, materialism, and amoralism.

What makes America's religion uniquely American and so out of sync with the remainder of all Westernized countries? Forty percent of all U.S. adults believe in a strictly creationist origin of man. Another 33%, think that humans evolved over millions of years but with God's guidance. 56%- 68% of church attending Protestant Americans believe in some version of the Creationist origin of man. 40% of Americans believe in the Earth Creation Story, that Earth is only 6,000 - 10,000 years old! The rest of the industrialized western cultures consistently survey out on the same questions at somewhere between 12-30%. (*Religion,* Gallup Historical Trends, 2023)

The second leg of Nation Building, **individual rights**, is the leg most indicative of the American Dream. Individuals, given the opportunity, with limited protections by Nation, could build a quality life with independence and success in their chosen life style and occupational endeavor, and in many cases could achieve immense riches. Individualism is not achievable without expressed protections from 'government' though. From the beginning it has always been the self-acknowledged responsibility of American government to protect the individual, through a multitude of protections, which might include free land, crop subsidies, bounties, police and military protections, safe working conditions, environmental protections, protections from unscrupulous practices of big business, etc.

Its My Life
It's my life and I'll do what I want Don't push me
It's my mind and I'll think what I want Its my life
It's my life and I'll do what I want And I can do what I want
It's my mind and I'll think what I want You can't tell me

It's my life and I'll do what I want I'll do what I want
(The Animals, 1965)

Every facet of governmental regulation is formulated, in some measure, to protect individual citizens or classes of citizens. The American Story is rich with stories of governmental protections for those who could not defend or speak for themselves. The American Story is equally rich in stories about its many egregious acts towards fellow Americans. In theory the individual reigns supreme. The downside of unbridled individualism though is entitlement. The American Story is replete with examples of the entitled engaging in horrible atrocities towards people it never viewed as belonging to 'Tribe', like the Chinese immigrants used as slave labor to build the railroads to advance entitled railroad barons, or Black slavery by entitled cotton barons, or limiting the rights of women by entitled men, or stories of the demise of the indigenous Indians by entitled government, internment of the Japanese during WWII, and on and on. The American Story touts equal protection without providing the means necessary to achieve protection and justice for African Americans, Women, Asians, Native Americans, Latino/Hispanic, and LGBT+. Protections and justice can not always be regulated nor legislated. We are not universally hard-wired by our biology to be able to accept that those not of our Tribe are entitled to the same protections and justice we take for granted/entitled.

Individualism/Entitlement has lead to the creation of America's out-of-control Litigious Society which has become the current American weapon of choice to effectively supplant the will of the majority. Entitlement now pervades every level of individualism in the American Story and is significantly responsible for the American Story now being more accurately portrayed as the American Malaise. Entitlement has its roots not in Nurture but in man's very Nature/Biology. Individual buy-in to the American Story implies an implicit understanding and expectation that as individuals we assume any goal is achievable. Given natural or learned ability one must also have equal opportunity to achieve, and there-in is the catch to the American Dream: A 2020 Gallup poll found 54% of respondents felt strongly the American Dream was unattainable to them.

Identity Crisis

Planet Earth has existed for 4.5 billion years. Modern humans (Homo sapiens) for a mere 300,000 years. If the earth's existence represents a twenty-four hour day, humans have dwelled here for approximately 3 seconds. We have not had the sufficient necessary eons to evolve into a species which prioritizes involvement in the attainment of the Greater Good. We are far removed from being able to consistently and routinely make moral judgments which benefit that Greater Good. Our Morality is still developing. We are still a hunter/nester species, fighting for day-to-day survival, guided by our Negativity Bias to stay alive. Our Amygdala stills rules over rational, non-emotive thought and decision-making.

In the 1997 movie, *The Devils Advocate,* Al Pacino, as John Milton aka the Devil, delivers a speech, parts of which have become as much an American idiom of the American Story in English lexicon as parts of Michael Douglas's speech became when he uttered "Greed Is Good" in his movie role in the 1987 film *Wall Street.*

Gordon Gekko (Michael Douglas):
"America has become a second rate power, …
… the new law of evolution in corporate America,
Seems to be survival of the unfittest …
The point is … **Greed is Good**,
Greed is right, it works, it clarifies, it captures
The American spirit. It marks the upward surge of mankind"

John Milton a la the Devil (Al Pacino):
God is a prankster …
He gives Man instincts,
… but he sets the rules in opposition …
Look don't touch, touch don't taste, taste don't swallow …
I'm a humanist, maybe the last humanist, who could possibly deny
The 20th century was entirely mine?

The Geologic Calendar uses a calendar year to map the geological lifetime of the Earth. On this calendar the first appearance of living single-celled organisms, prokaryotes, occurs on February 25 somewhere between 12:30 and 1:07 pm; dinosaurs first appeared on December 13, and the first primates on December 28 at about 9:43 pm. The first humans did not arrive until around 11:48 p.m. on December 31st. All of human history since the end of the last ice-age occurred in the last 82.2 seconds of the last calendar day of that year! And somehow we think we are in charge of defining our own way? It will take many more eons and not just a couple of generations to evolve into a more moral society, with an inherent interest in achieving the Greater Good for all; if that is even the direction we evolve. We are simply slaves to our genes; our bodies are here to service the genes which dictate our nature. Nurture determines the extent to which we actualize our nature. We do not determine the Tribe to which we belong. Our genes predispose us to our Tribe even though it is increasingly clear we have evolved to a point where there are just two primary tribes, with a multitude of many-mini-sub-tribes within each primary tribe. It is up to Nurture to actualize that assimilation.

America's biology is the major contributor to its unraveling and malaise; not its politics, not its religion and not its culture. It could not then, at America's inception, nor can it now, help itself. Its choice to devolve was not a conscious one for we can be no better or no worse at any given moment in time than our biology predisposes us to be! We are always doing the best we can, and that can be a very bitter pill to swallow and come to grips with! We are just not that much in control of our lives; our genes are!

America is genetically made up of at least two predominant Tribes, i.e., gene pools. Trying to combine those two Tribes into one nation might have worked better if the two tribes had existed in at least equal measure, but they did not populate America as equals. What we now refer to as Red America was seemingly then, and probably still is today, the larger of the two groups which we currently refer to as Red and Blue America, even though those two monikers are equally inaccurate. In truth when I speak to Red and Blue America I am more often than not referring to Red/Blue Extreme America (hyper-reactive, emotive and consciously unawares decision-making) vs Red/Blue Moderate (rational/non-emotive, thoughtful, yet slower decision-making) America.

Red/Blue Extreme America and Red/Blue Moderate America are much more fundamentally different in how they physiologically process information and make decisions than simply referring them as conservative/liberal, or Red/Blue America. We do a real disservice to those members of Red/Blue America who do lead proactive stories and who do strive to achieve the Greater Good when we simply clump them in with all the other members of singularly Red/Blue groups. As Twain reminds us, both conservative and liberal leaning people are generally quiet, respectful and generally see no point in standing up to or challenging the extremes of either Tribe, for example, being called out for being a Patriot or not?

It Is What It Is:

Twain: I know your race. It is made up of sheep. It is governed by minorities. Seldom or never by majorities. It suppresses its feelings and beliefs and follows the handful that makes the most noise. Sometimes the noisy handful is right. Sometimes wrong. But no matter, the crowd follows it. The vast majority of the race, whether savage or civilized are secretly kindhearted, and shrink from inflicting pain. But in the presence of the aggressive and pitiless minority they don't dare assert themselves. (*The Mysterious Stranger,* 1916)

Admittedly these two groups have always been simplistically described as conservative or liberal, Red or Blue. Unfortunately almost everything and anything written about these two groups speaks to the extreme edge of each group, has divided the two groups into those who are politically conservative and those who are politically liberal, pretty much along Party lines, leaving out the probable near-majority of each group which is nothing like the attention seeking extremists within each tribe. My own distinctions of the two founding gene pools will be as I have just distinguished them: Red/Blue Extreme America and Red/Blue Moderate America. This distinction better follows along with Ken Burns stating it is just a case of where do Americans want to live: Bedford Falls or Pottersville? Bedford Falls story would better align with Red/Blue Moderate America, while Pottersville's story would better align with Red/Blue Extreme America. The same alignment seems to coincide better with Saunders' distinction of the United States of Tom (Extreme) vs the United States of Huck (Moderate)?

Additional support for the veracity of this distinction is provided by work from the Hidden Tribes Project which reached essentially the same distinctions as I have adopted with Red/Blue Extreme America and Red/Blue Moderate America. The Hidden Tribes of America was a year long project launched by More in Common in late 2018 to better understand the forces that drive political polarization and tribalism in today's America. The Hidden Tribes study surveyed 8,000 Americans in 2017 and 2018 and identified seven Tribes, rather than the traditional two we have been operating under: Conservative/Liberal; Red/Blue; Democrat/Republican, etc..

Hidden Tribes' seven Tribes were grouped around shared beliefs and behaviors:

Progressive Activists - 8%
Traditional Liberals - 11%
Passive Liberals - 15%
Politically Disengaged - 26%
Moderates - 15%
Traditional Conservatives - 19%
Devoted Conservatives - 6%

The one furthest to the right, known as the Devoted Conservatives, (6%) hold the more uncompromising positions on political views and view themselves as the last defenders of America's 'traditional' values. The Progressive Activists (8%), more cosmopolitan and furthest to the left on issues of equity, fairness, and secularism, were by far the most prolific group on social media: 70 percent had shared political content over the previous year. The Devoted Conservatives followed, at 56 percent. These two extreme groups are similar in surprising ways. They are the whitest and richest of the seven groups, which suggests that America is being torn apart by a battle between two subsets of the elite who are not representative of the broader society. More evidence the extremes are more similar in how they think (hyper-reactive) then we previously thought (Self, *I Think, Therefore I Am*, 2022).

As it turns out though, the more religious, patriotic and highly moralistic Traditional Conservatives (19%) apparently are more similar than dissimilar in their views, just less intense, than Devoted Conservatives which allowed the Hidden Tribes project to better group the three more extreme groups into one group which they label The Wings (33%). "Combined, the members of these three tribes compromise just one-third of the population, but they often dominate our national conversation. Tribalism runs deep in their … hyper-reactive … thinking. Their distrust and fear of the opposing side drives many of the people in these groups, and they have especially negative opinions of each other." (Hidden Tribes Project, 2023). I will continue to use Red/Blue Extreme America to refer to the three Tribes of 'The Wings', and Red/Blue Moderate America to refer to the other four Hidden Tribes distinctions.

> "Nineteenth-century philosopher John Stuart Mill called it "commonplace" to have "a party of order or stability and a party of progress or reform." Ralph Waldo Emerson noted that "the two parties which divide the state, the party of conservatism and that of innovation, are very old, and have disputed the possession of the world ever since it was made." Emerson called this division "primal" and argued that "such an irreconcilable antagonism, of course, must have a correspondent depth of seat in the human condition. (Hibbing, J.R., et.al., *Predisposed*, p. 17, 2014.)

> "Liberals and conservatives often are reluctant to accept that their differences are rooted in psychology, let alone biology. Their own political beliefs seem so sensible, rational, and correct that they have difficulty believing that other people, if given full information and protected from nefarious and artificial influences, would arrive at different beliefs. (Hibbing, J.R., et.al., *Predisposed*, p. 17, 2014.)

And the reason we can conclude America was established with a disproportionate ratio of Red/Blue Extreme to Red/Blue Moderates? We look at what was 'Left Behind', predominantly in Europe and how they continued to develop with the same two gene pools from which settlers populated America. America and Europe continued evolving but in two dissimilar ways. America's devolvement is unique to America in comparison to its European-based 'parent pool'. We have Trumpism, a MAGA dichotomy, Far-right Evangelicals, beyond out-of-control gun rights advocates, a country of separate states passing disparate laws affecting LGBT+ rights, abortion rights, de facto segregationist treatment of blacks, etc.. Admittedly, European nations have pockets of the same issues but there is no evidence of across-the-board negative narratives which are driving the American Malaise. Descriptors of the 'Left Behind' Europeans include a nicer, less religious, more humanitarian view towards those not like them, where killing and violence are way down, with individuals less superficial, less materialistic and lack the insistence on individualism. There is a greater sense of Morality displayed by the Left Behinds! I also ran across the following study which tends to support the notion that the Left Behinds have developed a higher sense of morality than did their American counterparts : *"Good Manners, Obedience and Unselfishness: Data Reveals How UK Parenting Priorities Compare With Other Nations,* (*King's College of London, Sept., 2023*).

> "Changing attitudes towards parenting means the UK public now rank among the lowest internationally for the importance they place on obedience or responsibility in children, and among the highest for how much they value unselfishness, good manners and imagination…

> And while the vast majority of Britons have consistently said it is especially important for children to have good manners, this has declined in importance elsewhere, particularly in the US, where good manners are now valued the least out of 24 countries included in the research. The top traits Americans prioritized were tolerance, independence and diligence…

On several traits, Britons' views vary little by generation – with the exception of Gen Z, who stand out as least likely to say tolerance for other people and good manners are essential qualities in children."

And what about our neighbors to the north: our friends the Canadians. Have any off us ever heard any kind of negative reaction or comment about Canadians? I visited Canada as a college student and was instantly impressed with how clean the country was and how friendly all the Canadians with whom I interacted were. I have never talked with any Americans who had visited Canada or had interacted with Canadians who had anything other to say than how friendly and polite they were. Fifty years after my college experience in Canada my wife and I toured Canada on vacation a couple of times. On our most recent visit and in the name of doing research for this book, I sat down with a group of Canadian women and asked various questions about their impressions of Americans. Guns and violence were the first impressions they shared. When I asked what made Canadians and Americans different, their impressions were Canadians were friendlier and better mannered. Just like their UK counterparts, Canadians use and expect to be spoken to by those exhibiting good manners.

On 9/11 more than 250 International flights were forced to divert to Canada because of the closing of American airspace. Thirty-eight of those flights touched down that day at Gander International Airport in Newfoundland, Canada. After 24 hours stranded on their planes 7,000 off-loading passengers, and crew left the airport by school bus. Neither Appleton, with a population of just over 9,000, nor towns in the surrounding area had enough hotel space for the 7,000 stranded passengers. Local residents responded.

Area pharmacies filled prescriptions without cost, banks of free public telephones were installed so visitors could call home, and donations of toiletries, clothing, and food flowed in. Community television stations put out a call to "lend a hand, do what you can." Schools and nonessential businesses were closed, allowing Newfoundlanders ranging from senior citizens to schoolchildren to volunteer.

For five days, residents of that small town provided food, shelter and support to weary and worried international travelers. They offered such warmth and generosity that many friendships between residents and their guests continue today. After the passengers were finally able to return to America, the mayor of Appleton shared: "It was only natural for us to look after people who were in need of love and compassion, and food and clothing. Our people today still don't understand why it's such a big deal because it was … things that we do naturally."

The story was eventually turned into the Broadway play 'Come From Away'. The story is remarkable in its own right as a demonstration of the Canadian penchant for helping others, and more-so as an example of compassion for strangers of diverse ethnic origins, sexual orientation and religious affiliations. The compassion shown by Canadians begs the question: 'Would similar compassion have been shown by Americans in a similar situation?' Examples of such compassion surely exist in Blue America, with various religious and ethnic immigrant populations being assimilated in our larger cities and various Blue states. How might Red America have responded? By sending bus loads of immigrants to northern cities as the governors of Florida and Texas have done? How timely was the response to stranded Americans at the Super Dome post-Katrina? Where was our compassion during the January 6th insurrection?

Too Much?
That's Still The Point!
(Anthony Anderson)

And then there are these examples of simple traffic requests signs seen recently along Canadian highways **asking** for compliance; rather than **demanding obedience** (as US Highway signs do):

Canadian traffic signs:

<u>Truckers</u>   **Be Courteous**   **Merge Here**
Please Avoid   **Merge Traffic Ahead**   **Take Turns**
Use Of Engine
Retarder Brakes
Next 3km

American Jake Brake Signs, By Comparison:

Use Of   **Radar Enforced**   **Do Not**
Engine Brake   **No Engine Brake**   **Use Jake**
Retarder   **Brakes**
Jake Brake
Prohibited

Cynically-It-Is-What-It-Is speaking, the American Story, The American Way, The American Character and/or the American Malaise has devolved into something akin to Schizophrenia: **a serious cultural disorder in which people interpret reality abnormally, characterized by delusions: false beliefs not based in reality (or true facts), faulty thinking skills and grossly disorganized behavior. The leadership tasked with bringing the American Ideals to fruition were left to work with citizens who were not as morally evolved as the Founding Fathers had anticipated they might be. They were tasked to build one nation with residents from both Bedford Falls and Pottersville, who looked and acted a lot like Huck and Tom. Like mixing oil and vinegar! You get what you get, and it is what it is.**

Today, the American Story is in serious trouble. Emily Esfahan-Smith (*The Pursuit Of Meaning In Life,* PBS Newshour, March 2017): "We are in a crisis of despair. Wealth is up, poverty is down, yet suicides are up significantly, partly because we feel we have not made our lives count ...We have lost meaning and purpose!.... We have failed to realize that 'Belonging is the most essential source of meaning', that our story is not about us, but rather what we can give the world. We need to connect and contribute to see things beyond ourselves." **If 'belonging is the the most essential source of meaning', then the American Story is really about the significant numbers of all Americans, Red and Blue, who want and need nothing more than to belong and who hold differing versions of what belonging constitutes.** I again remind the reader we come into the world alone and we leave it alone, and in between we spend most of our lives attempting to convince ourselves we matter and as such we must **belong.** If we belong, then surely we are not alone? Does 'belonging' keep us from feeling alone? Each group now claims to be 'not feeling it (… allegiance to the story)'! Blue Americans: "If MAGA and Trumpism is what you're selling as the American Way, then I'm not buying", and conversely Red Americans respond with if "equality and fairness is what you're selling as the American Way then we ain't buying it either". Each group feels betrayed by their Tribe, which is really the same Tribe with two apparent faces? American stories built around character and experience define our place in the world, and many in Red and Blue America are experiencing a loss of 'character-driven place' resulting in despair. Instead of 'giving and belonging', it is more predominately about 'taking' through Entitlement and Individualism, making for a real disconnect with loss of integrity, morality, meaning and purpose!

Sandra Day O'Conner's
Final Words To Her Boys
Delivered At Her 2023 Memorial Service:
"Our Purpose In Life Is To
Help Others Along The Way"

I Am A Rock
I've built walls
A fortress deep and mighty
That none may penetrate
I have no need of friendship, friendship causes pain
It's laughter and it's loving I disdain
I am a rock I am an island
(Paul Simon, 1965)

It Is Not What You Want,
Its What You Give
(Crown Royal Commercial)

Anthony Anderson:
Too Much, That's the Point!

Too Much, ... how? Red/Blue Extreme Americans are lonely because they ...

..... view life as a glass half-empty. They feel a certain sense of entitlement which has not been delivered upon. They exemplify a pessimistic view towards everything and everybody. They view everyone as out to get them or cheat them; they indulge in conspiracy theories and will repeat any absurdity as evidence the World is out to cheat them. They do not trust Humanity, do not believe in a Greater Good, do not trust members of out-groups and they strongly resist change. When posed with involvement in any novel activity or idea their first reaction will be 'No', 'Yeah, but', 'Maybe', 'We'll see', and lots of negative non-verbal indicators like crossed arms, closed body positions, frowns and shrugs. There is no stopping and thinking about what is about to be said; responses are emotive, automatic and unfiltered.

.....view life through an experience filter as being black/white, right/wrong/, yes/no, either/or, with no ambiguity. Words used in any conversation are going to be taken literally, with no nuance nor ambiguity. They need the clear boundaries in order to make sense out of their experiences. To keep from having to think about the ambiguity which is life, they fall back on their religious beliefs to provide directions without question. Life is simpler this way.

.....view life as composed of Absolutes! Belief in, and adherence to the Absolutes keep folks from having to 'think': to think about the moral dilemmas the rest of us face and attempt to work through. God is an Absolute! Religion is an absolute. The Bible is the un-errant, literal word of God. Authority is an absolute; unwavering and undeniable! Rules are absolute and to be followed unquestionably. Loyalty is an absolute. The morality of this group is absolute and to be defended in all cases, even if irrefutable evidence questions the foundations of their morality. Adherence to the descriptors of my Tribe is paramount.

.....view life as full of conspiracies! Conspiracy theories flourish during times of crisis," says Joseph Pierre, psychiatrist and researcher at the David Geffen School of Medicine at UCLA. "When we feel insecure, we often look for information that provides an explanation for chaotic events." People seek out alternate takes on reality when they're inclined to mistrust official ones for various reasons. Groups most susceptible to conspiracy theories are those with lower socioeconomic status, those who have been excluded or ostracized and those who feel life is out of control. "When people feel powerless, anxious or threatened ... (i.e., hyper-reactive thinkers!)...," says Northumbria University social psychologist Daniel Jolley, "conspiracy theories can offer some relief." When you've been relegated to an out-group, it's easy to see conspiracy theories as the perfect antidote to exclusion. Research confirms that people adopt conspiracy beliefs as a way to feel unique. Conspiracy theories also stem from the very human tendency to look for patterns and broader meanings in the world. This tendency often promotes our survival as a species, and serves as a good example of the hyper-reactive's reliance on negativity bias.

..... acknowledge defining a portion of thinking as pattern detection, but in keeping with their negativity bias their thinking tends to focus initially and automatically on the exceptions to the patterns, whereas a proactive thinker tends to look for the patterns, whatever they may be and will intuitively match them to their already functioning schemata. For the proactive thinker the solution to any problem or question will typically spring forward out of their minds, fully formed, whereas the hyper-reactive thinker will first notice the exception and go with their instinctual gut level intuition without thinking everything through to completion (another example of the application of the negativity bias).

.....exercise a morality which is Tribal and inward-looking and supportive of 'Me' and/or 'Us'. Tribal morality protects in-group dynamics and does not consider change as positive.

..... are big on just 'being'. Little thought is given to who they 'are', who they might 'be', where they come from or their 'purpose', etc.. This attitude is a cultural credo or motto and best reflected in the song lyrics, 'Que sera, sera. Whatever will be, will be. The future's not ours to see, Que sera, sera.

.....exhibit the Type A behavior pattern. Type A behavior is a set of dominant behaviors and emotional reactions that include a high emphasis of competition, impatience, hostility and aggression. And those who might not be classic Type A, who view themselves as non-competitive, are still quick to anger, even to the point of deniability. Notably, the single most revealing aspect of Trump's election was his ability to tap into the deep wells of anger of the electorate and to have it turned loose by his supporters as the campaign progressed. Notable too in that people who most of us would never take for possessing, much less displaying anger routinely became hostile and angry in their replies to queries as to how they could support Trump.

.....are sticklers for rules. They believe in them, never question them and will make every effort to follow them. This is resultant of their reliance on lock-step, sequential logic. Engineers and military personnel are poster-child stereotypes of consummate rule followers. There is always one best way to do everything, and convergent thinking gets and keeps them there. They do not want to think about much outside their intellectual boundaries, do want to rely on the authority of the higher power and would not have the formal problem-solving skills to do so if they did happen to challenge a rule. Convergent thinking is the type of thinking that focuses on coming up with the single, best, time-worn answer to a problem. Convergent thinking emphasizes speed, accuracy, and logic and focuses on recognizing the familiar, reapplying techniques, and accumulating stored information. A critical aspect of convergent thinking is that it leads to a single best answer, leaving no room for ambiguity. In this view, answers are either right or wrong, black or white. Convergent thinking is the manipulation of existing knowledge and done so by manipulating that knowledge by means of standard procedures. This contrasts with divergent thinking where judgment is deferred while looking for and accepting many possible solutions (Wikipedia).

.....demonstrate an over-reliance on automaticity. Automaticity is the ability to do things without occupying the mind with the low-level details required, allowing it to become an automatic response pattern or habit. It is usually the result of learning, repetition, and practice. Tasks carried out by 'muscle memory' often involve some degree of automaticity, such as walking, speaking, bicycle-riding, assembly-line work, and driving a car. Most human behavior probably falls into automatic response behavior, not requiring any thought and fostering an over-reliance on 'habitual' thinking. Langer, Chanowitz and Blank conducted experiments on automaticity where their findings have shown how compliant people will be with requests which sound reasonable, but actually aren't.

Epilogue

And so now I arrive at my after-writing reflections.

What was my purpose for writing? How successful might I have been in choosing the best narrative to get my point across to others in the clearest terms possible? I will most likely never know how my choices might be received by the reader, unless you and I meet by happenstance someday and you share your thoughts?

My life goal has always been to live a life of meaning and integrity through story. I have always been fascinated by the power of story to shape lives, both for the good and for the worst. I have equally been fascinated by how story shapes our lives without our even knowing it. This then, was my purpose: To share the importance of meaningful stories if any form of meaning and purpose is what we might seek out of life? I know I am not the only one to accept the importance of story in shaping one's life?

> "If you can keep your head when all about you
> Are losing theirs and blaming it on you,
> If you can trust yourself
> when all men doubt you, …
> Yours is the Earth and everything that's in it,
> And - which is more -" …
> [Yours will have been a life filled with meaning and purpose]
> (Rudyard Kipling, *If: A Father's Advice to His Son*)

It certainly seems too many Americans are losing their heads and blaming it on others instead of taking a good look at themselves. We are a seriously divided nation and our uniquely American story is in serious crisis: Many would even say doomed! My hope has been to show at least one course through it. My path is just one of many proactive pathways for us to chart our story. My own path was defined for me many years ago by my circumstances. I shared those circumstances in the Preface and alluded back to them frequently throughout. I was fortunate enough to be 'listening' to the moral lessons behind those circumstances. I truly believe those circumstances were reflective of my genetic predispositions to strive towards a Greater Good.

Are there still occasions in which I feel an 'emptiness' in my life— sure!
Do I still get lonely? You bet!
Have I achieved 'belonging'?

Seems to me there remains an unanswerable question regarding what constitutes 'belonging'? It appears to have something to do with whatever it might be for which we are searching. If what we are ultimately searching for is acceptance to prove we are not alone, then we need 'to belong', yet how do we know when we have achieved it? If we achieve 'belonging' are we not still alone? Why else do I still have feelings of emptiness? Can any of us ever truly 'belong'? Does 'belonging' negate our loneliness? Isn't it enough to have achieved solitary meaning and purpose, I.e., Twain's Old Man:

> "This is the law, keep it in your mind. From the cradle to his grave a man never does a single thing which has any first and foremost object but one—to secure peace of mind, spiritual comfort, for **himself**: ... Man's sole impulse…(is)…the securing of his own approval."

I 'belong' to the Family of Man. I 'belong' to the species Homo sapiens. But those do not seem to provide purpose. Wouldn't a Christian who has been 'saved' truly believe they 'belong' to the family of Christ? Wouldn't soldiers and Seal Team members not be equally convinced they found 'belonging' as members of a Band of Brothers? Don't successful athletic teams who experience a common experience feel like they 'belong' to that experience? To me 'belonging' implies acceptance and reciprocity. I will continue to speculate whether or not 'belonging' can have both negative and positive perspectives? Belonging has a certain ring of selfishness associated with it: belonging seems to serve my needs rather than my living a life for others to serve the Greater Good.

So while my questions remain about 'belonging' I can still acknowledge my occasional feelings of emptiness and loneliness. But at least now I know the source of those feelings, and rather than letting them rule my life choices, I understand and accept them. They can no longer rule me. But overall the emptiness and loneliness I might still experience is so underwhelming as to be negligible. I view my story as having been charmed and blessed. I can look myself in the mirror each day and see my best version of integrity looking back at me! I am not so sure the 'belonging' issue is as important as in might seem to living any story with meaning and purpose, I.e., the pursuit of the Greater Good. I think Bessie Anderson Stanley and George Bernard Shaw would be pleased! I know I am. And I think most of you should be too!

Southern Cross
Think about how many times I have fallen,
Spirits are using me,
Larger voices calling
(Crosby, Stills and Nash)

My Way
And now the end is here
And so I face that final curtain
My friend I'll make it clear
I'll state my case, of which I'm certain
I've lived a life that's full
I traveled each and every highway
And more, much more
I did it, I did it my way
Regrets, I've had a few
But then again, too few to mention
(Frank Sinatra, 1969)

Live Long and Prosper
(Spock, CBS Studios),
Have a Good Life,
Strive for the Greater Good

Mike Self,
Christmas, 2023

References

….. (5/2022). US Department of the Interior Releases Report: Federal Indian Boarding School Initiative Investigative Report

….. (2023) Religion, Gallup Historical Trends

….. (9/2023). Good Manners, Obedience and Unselfishness: Data Reveals How UK Parenting Priorities Compare With Other Nations. King's College of London

Anderson, K. (2017) Fantasyland: How America Went Haywire. Random House: NY

Argyris, C. & D. Schon (1974) *Theory Into Practice, Increasing Professional Effectiveness.* Jossey-Bass: San Francisco

Bach, R. (1970). *Jonathan Livingston Seagull, A Story.* Avon Books: NY

Barry, C. & M. Wong, (8/2020). Fear of missing out (FoMO): A generational phenomenon or an individual difference?, Journal of Social and Personal Relationships

Burdick, E. & W. Lederer (1958) *The Ugly American.* Norton

Cole-Whittaker, T. (1988), What You Think Of Me Is None of My Business. Penguin Publishing: NY

Dean, R. (2006). The Value of Humanity in Kant's Moral Theory. Clarendon Press: Oxford

Devoto, B. (1962). *Mark Twain Letters from the Earth.* Harper & Row: NY

Esfahan-Smith, E. (3/2017). *The Pursuit Of Meaning In Life:* PBS Newshour

Fitzgerald, F.S. (1936). *The Crack-up:* New Directions Publishing

Frey, R. & Parker, K. (October 5, 2021). Rising Share Of U.S. Adults Are Living without a Spouse or Partner, PEW.

Gopnik, A. (2023). Pessimism Is the One Thing Americans Can Agree On, Wall Street Journal

Greene, J. (2013). Moral Tribes: Emotion, Reason, and the Gap Between Us and Them. Penguin Press: London

Gross, D. (11/2015) Smithsonian Magazine

Haidt, J. (5/2022). Why The Past Ten Years of American Life Have Been Uniquely Stupid, …It's not just a phase: The Atlantic

Hamblin-Hart, K. (3/2022). Making Meaning Of Our Lives through Stories: podcast

Harari, Y.N. (in Hebrew, 2011, and English, 2014). Sapiens, A Brief History Of Mankind. Dvir Publishing House: Israel; Random House: NY

Harris, T., (1969). I'm Ok, -You're Ok. Harper & Row: NY

Hawkins, S. (2018). Hidden Tribes Study. More In Common Project

Henderson, A. (1911). George Bernard Shaw: His Life and His Works. Cincinnati, Stewart, Kidd.

Hibbing. J.R., et.al. (2014). Predisposed,. Routledge: UK

Hiltzik, M. (4/2023). Column: America's decline in life expectancy speaks volumes about our problems, LA Times.

Kight, S. & Zachary Basu. (July 3, 2023). Americans are Down on Morality, Family and Country, Axios

Kuijsten, M. (2006). *Reflections on the Dawn of Consciousness.* Julian James Society: NV

Jaynes, J. The Origin of Consciousness in the Breakdown of the Bicameral Mind, Boston: Houghton Mifflin

Madison, J., (1788). Federalist #10, in The Federalist

Milbank, D. (3/2022) Opinion: Why do smart Republicans say stupid things?: The Washington Post

Murthy, Dr. V. (2023) Surgeon Generals Report, 2023

Newcomb, T. (4/8/2023). American IQ Scores Have Rapidly Dropped, Proving the 'Reverse Flynn Effect', Popular Mechanics

Nichols, T. (7/2022). Are the Last Rational Republicans in Denial? The current GOP is beyond rescue: Atlantic Daily

Nichols, T. (9/2023) When Americans Abandon the Constitution: Atlantic Daily

Nye, N.S., (2009) A poem in the Forward; Denied, Detained Deported, by Ann Bausem. National Geographic

Lang, B. (2022). Ken Burns' Urgent Warning: Why He is Scared For America's Future, Variety

Paka, M.M., (5/2023) American Genocide: the Crimes of National American Boarding Schools, Vanity Fair podcast

Powers, R. (2005). *Mark Twain, A Life.* Free Press: NY

Rodriguez, A. (2/2019). Storytelling Is a Different Story For Each Culture. Forbes

Saunders, G., (2007). The United States of Huck. *The Braindead Megaphone, Essays.* Riverhead Books: NY.

Self, M. (2020). *I Think, Therefore I Am, probably wrong!.* Palmetto Publishing Group: Charleston

Shaw, G. (1903). Man and Superman (1903).

Shmerling, R. (10/2022). Why Life Expectancy in the US is falling, Harvard Health Publishing: Cambridge

Smith, H.M. (1945). Henry VIII and the Reformation. Macmillan, London

Steiner, D. (July 20, 2023). America's Education System Is a Mess, and Its Students Who Are Paying the Price, The74

Thompson, D. (5/2022). This Is How America's Culture War Death Spirals. Why Disney vs. DeSantis is the Future of Politics: Atlantic

Tierney, J. & R. Baumeister, (2019). The Power of Bad: How Our Negativity Rules Us and How We Can Rule It. Allen Lane: London

Twain, M. (1910). What Is Man?. Watts and Co.:London. Pgs. 16 & 19

Twain, M. (1962). Letters From The Earth. Harper & Row: NY

Twain, M. (1916). The Mysterious Stranger. Harper and Brothers

Ware, B. (2011). The Top Five Regrets of the Dying. Hay House: Carlsbad, Ca.

About The Author

Mike is the son of a first generation immigrant mother from Russia and a military father whose own family came to America from Wales in 1792. Mike's father moved the family frequently and Mike eventually attended twelve different public schools before finishing high school. He has earned advanced degrees from the University of Alabama and completed a Post-Doctoral fellowship at UCLA.

A life-long Educator, Mike retired in 2012 as Director of The Harrell Learning Center, a Georgia public-school Psycho-Education Center working with Emotionally Conflicted children and youth, grades K-12. Mike has also spent nine years teaching and writing at the university level and has twenty-two years hands-on with students as a public school Principal.

He has previously published *The Conflict Resolution Curriculum for Children in Emotional Conflict* (1982), *I Think, Therefore I Am, probably wrong!* (2020), and is currently working on his next project, a parenting book for dads entitled *How To Raise a Happy Father.*

As a NASA-ASEE Summer Fellow he wrote on crew training programs for the Shuttle Program in 1981. His research interests have always revolved around student 'engagement' in active learning and efficient intellectual development for all learners.

After Mark Twain the major influences on his own 'conscious' efforts at proactive living include James Michener, Michael Crichton, Eric Berne, Stephen Covey and particularly Pat Conroy. And yes, Jonathan Livingston Seagull!

Milton Keynes UK
Ingram Content Group UK Ltd.
UKHW020955010424
440421UK00016B/1074